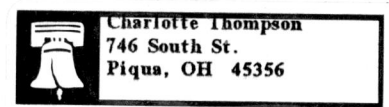

The Embattled Church

Colin D. Standish
President, Hartland Institute

and
Russell R. Standish
Founder, Remnant Ministries

Published and distributed by
Hartland Publications
P. O. Box 1
Rapidan, Virginia, 22733

Copyright © 1995 by Hartland Publications, Rapidan, VA.

Published in U.S.A.

ISBN 0-923309-29-2

The Church Embattled

1.	A Faltering Church	5
2.	Definitions and Speculation	11
3.	It Is Time to Seek a Pure Church	19
4.	Our Church—Is It the Remnant Church?	24
5.	The True Remnant	35
6.	The Flock and the Fold	42
7.	The Wheat and the Tares	47
8.	The Foolish Virgins	52
9.	The Sifting and the Shaking	57
10.	The Church Militant, The Church Triumphant	66
11.	Ancient Babylon and Ancient Israel	77
12.	Modern Israel and Modern Babylon	85
13.	The Loud Cry Message Is for Our Church	94
14.	Cast Out for Righteousness' Sake	101
15.	Church Discipline	108
16.	Organization, Structure, and Name	117
17.	Kingly Power	128
18.	When to Establish New Sabbath Schools and Companies	137

1
A Faltering Church

As we begin the seventh decade of our lives, we pause for deep reflection and evaluation of our own goals and of our dedication to God. The acknowledgment of our weaknesses and failures before the One we love brings us to the realization that every sentiment of our lives must be brought into conformity to the will of God. The burden for our own personal readiness to meet Jesus assumes even greater preeminence because of the times in which we live. So too does our burden grow for the Seventh-day Adventist Church which God has raised up to take the message of the everlasting gospel to every nation, kindred, tongue and people. This is no ordinary challenge. It is the greatest ever entrusted to any segment of the human race.

> In a special sense Seventh-day Adventists have been set in the world as watchmen and light bearers. To them has been entrusted the last warning for a perishing world. On them is shining wonderful light from the word of God. They have been given a work of the most solemn import—the proclamation of the first, second, and third angels' messages. There is no other work of so great importance. *They are to allow nothing else to absorb their attention*
> (*Testimonies*, vol. 9, p. 19, emphasis added).

Having been born into an undivided Seventh-day Adventist home, we have known nothing but the Seventh-day Adventist Church. It is the church with the message that led our maternal grandmother and our paternal great-grandfather at great sacrifice and risk to acceptance, because they knew it was God's message. This is the church to which our parents taught us to be faithful and loyal. It was God's church with God's truth to be given to the world so that the coming of Jesus might become a reality.

Growing up in the Seventh-day Adventist Church, we could only assume that those who were not Seventh-day Adventists either were ignorant of the Seventh-day Adventist truth, or they had blatantly rejected it. Following the counsel and entreaties of our parents, this is the church to which we dedicated our lives in service. Never for a moment have we ever regretted following God's leading. Except for our loyalty to God and His Son, and the promptings of the Holy Spirit and the ministry of the inspired Word, the Seventh-day Adventist Church has held the highest authority in our lives.

Our parents were willing to sacrifice financially, and if need be, scholastically that we might obtain a Christian education. In the home, in the school, in the church, and in evangelistic crusades we heard nothing that would have caused uncertainty in our hearts and lives. It seemed to us that the Seventh-day Adventist message pulsated with such authenticity that there could be no "ifs, buts or maybes." Had we been asked to evaluate our local church we are sure that we would have confidently asserted that at least ninety percent of our church members were heaven-bound. We failed to realize that our church had yet to be tested, tried and proved. The results of later tests would create a shocking schism beyond any possible expectation that we had or could have had.

Of course we had heard the warnings of the great separation to come; the sifting and the shaking; especially in the readings of the annual weeks-of-prayer. But somehow the immensity and the reality of this did not penetrate to any great depths of our consciousness. Our church seemed too secure, too certain, too unwavering for more than a handful to be torn by anything that Satan might thrust at it. But how wrong we were!

In our childhood and early youth we had the privilege of attending the regular six-month-long crusades that were held in our city and its suburbs annually. We attended because our parents were dedicated to faithfully supporting every crusade that was held. Thus year in and year out, we heard the mighty truths that make Seventh-day Adventism what it is. We received a grounding in God's truth that few youth today have been privileged to experience. Those of our generation who have grown in the church must surely agree that there has been a dramatic revolution in God's church, away from the mighty truths that were consistently taught many decades ago.

No longer does our church at any level pulsate with harmony. But rather division, differences, debates and schisms are to be found at all levels of our work. Assurance of truth has surrendered to uncertainty. Surety of faith has given way to an enfeebling pluralism. Distinctiveness has faltered before ecumenism. Righteousness has been engulfed by wickedness. Urgency has been replaced by carnal security. The spiritual church has become a social club. Unwavering loyalty is now branded as bigotry. Faithfulness to Christ is judged to be legalism. The defenders of the truth are spurned as schismatics. Like myriads of Seventh-day Adventist Church members, we are bewildered and stunned by this tragedy of tragedies. One aspect of this sweeping apostasy is that only once in the previous history of the Seventh-day Adventist Church has the leadership not risen up to defend truth and righteousness. That occurred in 1888. Today that same failure is being repeated more emphatically.

In 1888 the top leaders, George Butler, General Conference president, and Uriah Smith, Editor of *The Review and Herald*, united in an unholy alliance against the testimony of God through the servant of the Lord. At other times the leadership has been quick to denounce heresy and wickedness. At the time of the early apostasies such as the Marion Party and the Messenger Party, the denunciations of errors and the defense of truth were rapid and effective. The defection of men such as Canright, Kellogg, Ballenger, Jones, Conradi, Fletcher, Greive and others was met head-on and successfully, under the guidance of leadership. But sad to say, in the current crisis in our church, as in 1888, many of our top leaders have joined the rebellion against God's truth. The warnings had been clear.

> No superiority of rank, dignity, or worldly wisdom, no position in sacred office, will preserve men from sacrificing principle when left to their own deceitful hearts. Those who have been regarded as worthy and righteous prove to be ring leaders in apostasy and examples in indifference and in the abuse of God's mercies   (*Testimonies*, vol. 5, p. 212).

> It is with reluctance that the Lord withdraws His presence from those who have been blessed with great light, and who have felt the power of the Word in ministering to others. They were once His faithful servants, favored with His presence and guidance; but they departed from Him and led others into error, and therefore are brought under the divine displeasure
> (Ibid).

> The ancient men [church pastors] . . . had betrayed their trust
> (*Testimonies*, vol. 5, p. 211).

We have been warned that there will be apostasy at all levels of our work. The evidence that at least some leaders are responsible in supporting great deviation from truth can be found in the book, *Issues: The Seventh-day Adventist Church and Certain Private Ministries*, Review and Herald 1992, and in the *Adventist Review Insert*, November 5, 1992, *Issues: The Seventh-day Adventist Church and Certain Private Organizations*. Both were "Authorized by the officers and union presidents of the North American Division of the General Conference of Seventh-day Adventists."

On page eight of the *Adventist Review* insert, when talking about the "pivotal doctrines, such as victorious Christian living, the nature of Christ, and the atonement," the authors had this to say: "The united church in session has deliberately chosen to leave some points open because general agreement on specifics does not exist." They asserted, "The standard of Adventism must be a decision of the united Seventh-day Adventist Church in General Conference session" (ibid.). This is a most dangerous deviation from the principles of Seventh-day Adventism, which declare that the Bible and the Bible only is the basis of our faith and practice.

> God will have a people upon the earth to maintain the Bible, and the Bible only, as the standard of all doctrines and the basis of all reforms. The opinions of learned men, the deductions of science, the creeds or decisions of ecclesiastical councils, as numerous and discordant as are the churches which they represent, the voice of the majority—not one nor all of these should be regarded as evidence for or against any point of religious faith. Before accepting any doctrine or precept, we should demand a plain "Thus saith the Lord" in its support (*The Great Controversy*, p. 595).

Further, the authors of *Issues* assert,

> The real problem is that Hope International/*Our Firm Foundation* hold certain views on the nature of Christ, the nature of sin, and sanctification. These issues have never been settled among Christians, much less among Seventh-day Adventists. They are not issues so essential to salvation that souls will be

lost unless they are resolved. The problem that Hope International/*Our Firm Foundation* has created is that this independent ministry feels driven to charge the SDA Church with being in a state of apostasy because it does not accept their views on these moot theological issues (*Issues: The Seventh-day Adventist Church and Certain Private Ministries*, p. 109.4).

The doctrines pinpointed in these excerpts hit at the very heart of the preparation of God's people for the coming of Jesus. The issues of victorious Christian living, of the human nature of Christ, of sanctification, and the nature of sin are intimately bound to the message of Christ Our Righteousness; the message of the final atonement is the central theme of the sanctuary message which is the center of our faith (*The Great Controversy*, p. 488). Certain leaders have chosen to trivialize the very heart of the Seventh-day Adventist message dealing with the preparation of God's people for the return of their blessed Lord. Clearly those who have a love for God, His Word and His church cannot remain silent when such bold apostasies are declared, no matter if they have been supported by some in high ecclesiastical authority. Indeed, the demand to "Cry aloud" is the more urgent because it is men of profound influence who have dared to boldly and publicly promote shameful apostasy.

What could have caused such apostasy to reach even the highest level of God's work? The servant of the Lord leaves us in no doubt. The causes include:

1) Trust to intellect and science falsely so called
   (*Testimonies*, vol. 5, p. 80).
2) Self-sufficiency and independence of God   (ibid.).
3) A failure to develop a love for the truth
   (*Testimonies*, vol. 6, p. 401).
4) That having great light and precious privileges, these have not been improved. There has been no effort to live by every word that proceedeth out of the mouth of God
   (*Testimonies*, vol. 6, p. 132).
5) More interest has been displayed in the pursuits of the world than in the pursuit of Christ and His kingdom
   (*Testimonies*, vol. 5, p. 457).

6) There is a love for the prosperity of the world
(Testimonies, vol. 5, p. 456).
7) As part of the superficial conservative class, there has developed a sympathy with the avowed enemies of truth
(Testimonies, vol. 5, p. 463).

The magnitude of the apostasy and the complicity of not a few leaders in support and advancement of the cause of apostasy has created the greatest crisis in the history of the Seventh-day Adventist Church. It has resulted in a confusion which is of monumental magnitude. It has led untold thousands to reevaluate their relationship to the Seventh-day Adventist Church organization, and to question that a church in such apostasy could ever succeed in bringing the truth of God to the attention of every inhabitant of the world. This has stimulated the greatest separationist movement ever known in our ranks. This movement is worldwide. Many have lost all hope that the end-time message of God can ever be completed by the Seventh-day Adventist Church. Thus many have concluded that they must honor God by separating from an organization which no longer offers any hope to them of being the long-looked-for church that will transport God's people into the kingdom of heaven. It is to this issue of separation that this book is addressed.

Believing that the Seventh-day Adventist Church is now beyond all hope, these folk are forced to look for another church through which God will ultimately fulfill His promise to modern Israel to pour out His Holy Spirit in latter rain power, to give the loud cry to the world, to bring in everlasting righteousness and to be ready for the coming of the Lord. Thus we enquire, has God written "Ichabod" across the portals of the Seventh-day Adventist Church? Must we look for another? The word of inspiration answers these questions with unerring accuracy.

2
Definitions and Speculation

The question "What is the church?" has become the focal concern of many Seventh-day Adventists. Until recent times, the understanding of the nature of the church was taken for granted. There was little question in the minds of any faithful Seventh-day Adventists that the true church was the Seventh-day Adventist Church. This was God's church. It was raised up at a special time, with a special destiny, to do a special work. Few questioned that the Seventh-day Adventist Church was the last church; the church that would receive the latter rain, that would give the loud cry and would take the invitation of Jesus to every nation, kindred, tongue, and people through the proclamation of the everlasting gospel.

It was not that members did not recognize that there were hypocrites in the church. It was understood that as a people, we were not yet ready to be trusted with the latter rain. But the hope was firm in the breasts of most members that soon the perfect unity that is spoken of in both the Bible and the Spirit of Prophecy would be achieved. Unfortunately, most thought very little, or at least inadequately, about the work that needed to be done in their own lives as a prerequisite to their own readiness to receive the latter rain and to be part of that final generation that would take the gospel to every nook and cranny of the world.

It was as if we expected that God would wave a magic wand and all the wrongs and inadequacies of the church, its leadership and its members would vanish away and God would impose perfection upon His people. Because of this failure to sense the desperate need in their own spiritual lives, instead of the membership developing into a purer and holier people, the inadequacy of our Christian experience has led to a rapid increase in apostasy and wickedness in our ranks. Each member must recognize that the degree to which he or she has fallen short has contributed to the spiritual ineptitude within our church.

How often we look at the church as if it were apart and independent from ourselves and we blame "the church" inadvertently for what is taking place. In reality, each member of the church must assume a degree of responsibility for the malignant cancer of sin that has metastasized throughout the ranks of God's people. How many of us have followed the example of the prophet Daniel and prayed as he prayed?

> And I set my face unto the Lord God, to seek by prayer and supplications, with fasting, and sackcloth, and ashes: and I prayed unto the LORD my God, and made my confession, and said, O Lord, the great and dreadful God, keeping the covenant and mercy to them that love him, and to them that keep his commandments; *we have sinned, and have committed iniquity, and have done wickedly, and have rebelled, even by departing from thy precepts and from thy judgments*: neither have we hearkened unto thy servants the prophets, which spake in thy name to our kings, our princes, and our fathers, and to all the people of the land
> (Daniel 9:3–6, emphasis added).

In this moral and spiritual crisis, it is not a time to wring our hands or to concentrate the blame upon others, but to recognize that in our own personal lives we have contributed to the situation within our church. Some of us will hasten to point out that we have not deviated from the great truths that God has entrusted to the church. We have often thought to blame others for the problems which are in the church. True, some seem to have deliberately urged and manipulated to advance certain apostate teachings or practices within the church. Often, it is to leaders or pastors that such finger-pointing is directed. And truly, many have not been without serious guilt. There *is* a need to directly address such error.

There *is* a need to point out sin and the source of it in our church. However, let us be careful lest in so doing we forget that we ourselves have all too frequently fallen short of the glory of God. We must not be diverted from our own personal preparation for the kingdom of heaven, by developing a smug security that in the end may lead us away from our own heart preparation so necessary for the coming of our Lord and Saviour, Jesus Christ.

Many are uncertain as to the future of God's remnant church. Some, as stated in Chapter 1, have settled the issue by being convinced that the Seventh-day Adventist Church is no longer God's church. "Ichabod" has been written across the portals of

Definitions and Speculation 13

the Church. Such believe that a new church must emerge from the ashes of Seventh-day Adventism. Others have concluded that the true Seventh-day Adventist Church comprises only those who are true and faithful at this time. All others are not considered to be part of the church though they may have membership in a Seventh-day Adventist congregation. Others hold tenaciously to the conviction that irrespective of the rampaging apostasy within the church, all is well in Zion, and they comfort themselves by statements which minimize the degree of apostasy.

For example, in the tithe supplement in the *Adventist Review*, November 1991, appeared this statement. "No person acquainted with the Seventh-day Adventist Church would deny that throughout our history some apostasy has existed in our ranks—and does even today." That statement is a classic case of presenting facts in a way that greatly diminishes the reality of the situation. One of the most tragic dangers within the Seventh-day Adventist Church today is that so many tend to minimize the depth and the extent of apostasy, sin and worldliness. By so doing, they lose credibility with those who have been greatly burdened by the widespread rebellion in God's church. Yet those who are seeking to confine the church to one precise definition can do so only by a selective choice of references from Inspiration. Both the Bible and the Spirit of Prophecy use the word *church* in a number of different ways. Sometimes the word *church* refers to a building.

> But if there be no interpreter, let him keep silence in the *church*; and let him speak to himself, and to God
> (1 Corinthians 14:28, emphasis added).

> Schools are to be established in various places, publications are to be multiplied, *churches* are to be built in the large cities, and laborers are to be sent forth, not only into the cities, but into the highways and hedges
> (*Testimonies*, vol. 5, p. 382, emphasis added).

Sometimes the *church* is referred to as a local congregation.

> Likewise greet the *church* that is in their house
> (Romans 16:5, emphasis added).

> The *churches* of Asia salute you
> (1 Corinthians 16:19, emphasis added).

> And to our beloved Apphia, and Archippus our fellow soldier, and to the *church* in thy house (Philemon 2, emphasis added).

> The members of the *church* should individually hold themselves and all their possessions upon the altar of God
> (*Testimonies*, vol. 5, p. 465, emphasis added).

The church is also called the corporate body of Christ around the world.

> Husbands, love your wives, even as Christ also loved the *church,* and gave himself for it
> (Ephesians 5:25, emphasis added).

> That he might present it to himself a glorious *church*, not having spot, or wrinkle, or any such thing; but that it should be holy and without blemish (Ephesians 5:27, emphasis added).

> And he is the head of the body, the *church*: who is the beginning, the firstborn from the dead; that in all things he might have the preeminence (Colossians 1:18, emphasis added).

> Nothing else in this world is so dear to God as His *church*
> (*Testimonies*, vol. 6, p. 42, emphasis added).

Sometimes the church is depicted as a defective church.

> And all the brethren which are with me, unto the *churches* of Galatia. . . . I marvel that you are so soon removed from him that called you into the grace of Christ unto another gospel: which is not another; but there be some that trouble you, and would pervert the gospel of Christ
> (Galatians 1:2, 6, 7, emphasis added).

> And to the angel of the *church* in Pergamos write. . . . I have a few things against thee, because thou hast there them that hold the doctrine of Balaam, who taught Balac to cast a stumbling block before the children of Israel, to eat things sacrificed unto idols, and to commit fornication. So hast thou also them that hold the doctrine of the Nicolaitans, which thing I hate (Revelation 2:12, 14, 15, emphasis added).

> And unto the angel of the *church* in Thyatira write. . . . Notwithstanding I have a few things against thee, because thou sufferest that woman Jezebel, which calleth herself a

Definitions and Speculation 15

> prophetess, to teach and to seduce my servants to commit fornication, and to eat things sacrificed unto idols
> (Revelation 2:18, 20, emphasis added).

> And unto the angel of the *church* in Sardis write. . . . I have not found thy works perfect before God
> (Revelation 3:1, 2, emphasis added).

> And unto the angel of the *church* of the Laodiceans write. . . . I know thy works, that thou art neither cold nor hot: I would thou wert cold or hot. So then because thou art lukewarm, and neither cold nor hot, I will spue thee out of my mouth. Because thou sayest, I am rich, and increased with goods, and have need of nothing; and knowest not that thou are wretched, and miserable, and poor, and blind, and naked
> (Revelation 3:14–17, emphasis added).

> Christ saw how the existence of false brethren in the *church* would cause the way of truth to be evil spoken of. . . . Because these sinners were in the *church*, men would be in danger of thinking that God excused their sins
> (*Christ's Object Lessons*, p.122–123, emphasis added).

When Sister White wrote the *Testimonies to the Church*, she was not addressing a perfect church. Rather was she addressing our church as one full of almost every conceivable folly, apostasy and failure. If she was providing such testimonies to a church composed of pure Christians, then her nine volumes were an utter waste of effort.

Both the Bible and the Spirit of Prophecy also speak of a perfect church.

> And to her was granted that she should be arrayed in fine linen, clean and white: for the fine linen is the righteousness of saints (Revelation 19:8).

> That he might present it to himself a glorious *church*, not having spot, or wrinkle, or any such thing; but that it should be holy and without blemish (Ephesians 5:27, emphasis added).

> God has a *church*. It is not the great cathedral, neither is it the national establishment, neither is it the various denominations; it is the people who love God and keep His commandments (*Upward Look*, p. 315, emphasis added).

From the beginning, faithful souls have constituted the *church* on earth (*Acts of the Apostles*, p. 11, emphasis added).

Inspiration has also described the church in universal terms.

> The *church* of God below is one with the *church* of God above. Believers on the earth and the beings in heaven who have never fallen constitute one *church*. Every heavenly intelligence is interested in the assemblies of the saints who on earth meet to worship God
> (*Testimonies*, vol. 6, p. 366, emphasis added).

From another perspective the church is described as the "church militant."

> Let everyone who is seeking to live a Christian life, remember that the *church* militant is not the *church* triumphant. Those who are carnally minded will be found in the *church*. They are to be pitied more than blamed. The *church* is not to be judged as sustaining these characters, though they are found within her borders. Should the *church* expel them, the very ones who found fault with their presence there, would blame the *church* for sending them adrift in the world; they would claim that they were treated unmercifully
> (*Review and Herald*, January 16, 1894, emphasis added).

> Has God no living *church*? He has a *church,* but it is the *church* militant, not the *church* triumphant. We are sorry that there are defective members. . . . While the Lord brings into the *church* those who are truly converted, Satan at the same time brings persons who are not converted into its fellowship. While Christ is sowing the good seed, Satan is sowing the tares. There are two opposing influences continually exerted on the members of the *church*. One influence is working for the purification of the *church,* and the other for the corrupting of the people of God
> (*The Faith I Live By,* p. 305, emphasis added).

> Some people seem to think that upon entering the *church* they will have their expectations fulfilled, and meet only with those who are pure and perfect. They are zealous in their faith, and when they see faults in *church* members, they say, "We left the world in order to have no association with evil characters, but the evil is here also;" and they ask, as did the servants in the parable, "From whence then hath it tares?" But we need

> not be thus disappointed, for the Lord has not warranted us in coming to the conclusion that the *church* is perfect; and all our zeal will not be successful in making the *church* militant as pure as the *church* triumphant
> (*Testimonies to Ministers,* p. 47, emphasis added).

> We wish we had heaven here below, but we have not. The *church* militant is not the *church* triumphant. The *church* militant must wrestle and toil. She must strive against temptations and fight severe battles, because Satan is not dead. His agencies are much more active in his work than are the agencies of God in the work of their Leader (*General Conference Bulletin,* April 22, 1901, emphasis added).

However, the words of Inspiration also address the church triumphant.

> Continuing to resist the enemy, we shall constantly gain strength, and finally become the *church* triumphant
> (*Signs of the Times,* June 10, 1903, emphasis added).

> The life of Christ was a life charged with a divine message of the love of God, and He longed intensely to impart this love to others in rich measure. Compassion beamed from His countenance, and His conduct was characterized by grace and humility, love and truth. Every member of His *church* militant must manifest the same qualities, if he would join the *church* triumphant (*Our High Calling,* p. 366, emphasis added).

In these perilous times it is essential to be careful not to seek one simplistic definition of the church. That would be to deny the wide scope of meanings of the church as used in Inspiration, and would be sure to lead us away from the correct understanding of our personal relationship to the Seventh-day Adventist Church. There are those who are too eager to define the church only in terms of a pure and truth-believing people. But that is not a faithful definition of the present-day church, according to the Word of God. Since the creation of man, only before the fall was there a perfect church, unless for the briefest period at the time of the Noachian flood. Since then there have been defective members in God's church; whether that church be the nation of Israel, the Jewish church or the Christian church, or more specifically today the Seventh-day Adventist Church. There has never been a time when there have not been defective members in the church.

Those who believe the time has come to disassociate themselves from the Seventh-day Adventist Church to form a perfect church that will follow God in truth and righteousness will soon be disillusioned, for such a church is not possible until the completion of the shaking, when every tare has been gathered into bundles by the angels, ready for the great conflagration. Then, and then alone, will there be a perfect church on earth. But that perfect church, united with the perfect church of the universe, will never falter or fail again.

There is another group who emphasize the defectiveness of the church, and seem content to passively accept the terrible inroads into the Seventh-day Adventist Church of Catholic principles, spiritualistic and New Age concepts, and abominations of almost every kind. They are just as misguided in their understanding of the church as those who emphasize the monistic concept of a perfect church.

Putting aside the concept of the church as a building or a local congregation, and looking at the church from the perspective of the global church, the emphasis of Inspiration is clear. Short of the completion of the sifting and the shaking, the church will be an admixture of faithful and unfaithful members. Only at the close of human probation, when God has cleansed His church, will it be a perfect church. The church militant will have become the church triumphant. But that leaves other questions in the minds of concerned brethren and sisters. How far into apostasy does the church have to go before it is no longer God's church? How deep has to be the support of such apostasy by large segments of leadership and the pastoral ministry before the church becomes so corrupted that the only safe thing to do is to separate completely from the church rather than be associated with its abominations and be held responsible for its iniquities?

3

It Is Time to Seek a Pure Church

So defective has the Seventh-day Adventist Church become, so far removed from pure and holy standards, so accepting of apostate doctrines, so disinclined to preach our distinctive doctrines; so secularized have become our educational and medical institutions and so shameful are the contents of many publications issuing from our presses that it is time to seek a pure church. There can be no doubt whatsoever that the Seventh-day Adventist Church has mired itself in the omega of apostasy and it must be evident to all true believers that the church in its present organization cannot go through to the end. It just cannot do so!

Thus it is time to seek toward a pure church *now*. Let there be no further delay. Many Seventh-day Adventists, faithful to God's end-time message have joined us in this quest. Some have eschewed all relationship with the Seventh-day Adventist Church and have commenced single congregational churches. In these they have found a solution to their quest. We have chosen not to follow such a course for reasons which will be developed in subsequent chapters. One tremendous problem is that such an isolated congregation can not be seriously expected to proclaim this pure faith worldwide.

A much more appropriate response, and one with a better destiny, has been adopted by believers who have either been cast out of the Seventh-day Adventist Church because of their pure faith, or who can no longer permit their own souls and those of their children to be polluted by blasphemous worship services, the preaching of apostate doctrines and the practice of disgraceful worldly standards. They have chosen to remain Seventh-day Adventists, irrespective of the vote of their churches, to proudly and sincerely proclaim their denominational affiliation and to commence branch Sabbath Schools or to plant new church companies where truth and righteousness are proclaimed. While it is a rare experience for such branch Sabbath Schools or church companies to be accorded recognition as true Seventh-day Adventist entities by Seventh-day Adventist Church officialdom, nevertheless these members are wholly loyal to God's church in the real sense of the word. Our use of the term "God's Church" most emphatically must not be equated with the organization, where many administrators have earned no loyalty whatsoever. Those faithful still seek to witness to their fellow believers in the Seventh-day Adventist Church, they seek to assist in every pure enterprise, they genuinely cry and sigh for the Church and its members.

But is there a better solution even than this? Should we not seek for a church, already established world-wide, one which upholds true Seventh-day Adventist doctrines, one which eschews worldly standards, which proclaims the three angels' messages, one which would lead our young people along godly lines, where the Sabbath is revered and God's law and grace upheld?

We, ourselves, have found more than one such church. We have been drawn to their members and pastors and we have found much common ground for fellowship. The love of God has been evident in their lives. Many Seventh-day Adventists have been similarly drawn. But we have been hesitant to join their churches as members. We have remained Seventh-day Adventists.

The reason we have evidenced such reluctance is because the Spirit of Prophecy has declared that these churches, claiming to be God's genuine last day churches have been described as being overwhelmed by apostasy.

> The leaven of godliness has not entirely lost its power. At the time when the danger and depression of the church are greatest, the little company who are standing in the light will be sighing and crying for the abominations that are done in the land. But more especially will their prayers arise in behalf of the church, because its members are doing after the manner of the world (*Testimonies,* vol. 5, p. 209, 210).

The few genuine members in these churches cry for their overwhelming corruptness.

> They mourn before God to see religion despised in the very homes of those who have had great light. They lament and afflict their souls because pride, avarice, selfishness, and deception of almost every kind are in the Church. The Spirit of God, which prompts to reproof, is trampled under foot, while the servants of Satan triumph. God is dishonored, the truth made of none effect (Ibid. p. 210, 211).

Their pastors, in general, are a disgrace to their God-given duties.

> The ancient men [pastors], those to whom God had given great light and who had stood as guardians of the spiritual interests of the people, had betrayed their trust (ibid., p. 211).

These pastors do not honor their trust; indeed the Spirit of Prophecy condemns them:

> Thus peace and safety is the cry from men who will never again lift up their voice like a trumpet to show God's people their transgressions and the house of Jacob their sins. These dumb dogs that would not bark are the ones who feel the just vengeance of an offended God (ibid.).

Furthermore, these churches are concealing the most despicable evils.

> The abominations for which the faithful ones were sighing and crying were all that could be discerned by finite eyes, but by far the worst sins, those which provoked the jealousy of the pure and holy God, were unrevealed (ibid.).

Should any Seventh-day Adventist join such a church when such is God's description of them?

Many readers will no doubt resent the application which we have made of this passage from the Spirit of Prophecy. In some it may have generated a spirit of hostility. But we must stand by this identification, for these churches claim to be the remnant church, and this is the description of God's last day church. It applies to none other.

Many may protest that this is not in the least an accurate description of these reformed churches, but rather, faithfully depicts the present condition to be found in the regular Seventh-day Adventist Church. It will be asserted that we have misapplied the writings of the Spirit of Prophecy and applied them to churches which are far holier.

But this depiction, we insist, is found in the *"Testimonies to the Church"*—God's true church. These testimonies are not written for the fallen churches of Babylon. They are not written to a church which God has rejected. If these reform churches insist that they constitute God's last day church and that God rejected the Seventh-day Adventist Church, then they must examine themselves and identify the very reason why God has written such a scathing evaluation of *them*. If they deny that these words of severe denunciation apply to them, then they are plainly denying that they constitute God's last church. Until the sealing is completed, no church dare make a claim to be purer than God declares it to be, while purporting to be God's true church.

Of course, in all honesty, we must confess with deep remorse that the description which we have quoted from pages 209–211 of the fifth volume of the *Testimonies to the Church* applies to the Seventh-day Adventist Church. It most certainly does not refer to these reformed churches which contain so many earnest and dedicated members and pastors. Yet the unassailable fact is that the servant of the Lord informed us God's true church would experience such a decline as we now see. Nothing more clearly delineates God's church as the Seventh-day Adventist Church of the last decade of the twentieth century, than the fact that our church tragically fulfills every one of these specifications. It would thus be perilous to voluntarily leave God's church and join another, even if we do find it necessary to commence a branch Sabbath School or to seed a new company of believers for valid reasons. That Sabbath School or that company will be a Seventh-day Adventist entity in the truest sense and we will still identify ourselves, not as separate from God's severely faulted church, but as a part of it, just as Daniel did in his prayer of Daniel chapter 9.

Many do not perceive the implications of the sealing message of Ezekiel chapter 9.

> And the Lord said unto him, Go through the midst of the city, through the midst of Jerusalem, and set a mark upon the foreheads of the men that sigh and that cry for all the abominations that be done in the midst thereof. And to the others he said in mine hearing, Go ye after him through the city, and smite: let not your eye spare, neither have ye pity: slay utterly old and young, both maids, and little children, and women: but come not near any man upon whom is the mark; and begin at my sanctuary. Then they began at the ancient men which were before the house (Ezekiel 9:4–6).

Commenting on this passage Sister White plainly identifies Jerusalem as the church to which she is sending these testimonies—the Seventh-day Adventist Church.

> Here we see that the church—the Lord's sanctuary—was the first to feel the stroke of the wrath of God
> *(Testimonies, vol. 5, p. 211).*

Yet at the time of the sealing, both those who are sealed by the mark from the writer's inkhorn and those who will be slaughtered by God's avengers will be found within the city of Jerusalem, God's Seventh-day Adventist Church.

Those receiving the seal may have had their names unjustly and cynically cast off the membership list of their churches, but they will never create or join a new organization, for this is contrary to the expressed counsel of the Spirit of Prophecy, no matter how we may attempt to explain away that counsel.

> The Lord has declared that the history of the past shall be rehearsed as we enter upon the closing work. Every truth that He has given for these last days is to be proclaimed to the world. Every pillar that He has established is to be strengthened. We cannot now step off the foundation that God has established. We cannot now enter into any new organization; for this would mean apostasy from the truth
> *(Selected Messages, book 2, p. 390).*

As we shall see, our God has promised to gather together into His fold once more, those whom unfaithful shepherds have expelled.

Yes, it is time for God's children to seek toward a pure church. It is time to pray that the shaking process, now so near finality, will be completed so that God may have His church which is "found of him in peace, without spot, and blameless" (2 Peter 3:14). In that church will be found all who are righteous members of the Seventh-day Adventist Church. In that day they will be united with those faithful in the reformed churches, for all corrupt organization will be swept away as we flee to the mountain fastnesses.

We now live in very perplexing times, but a faithful search of God's Word will bring certainty of course and faithfulness of service in these perilous times. Soon the faulted church militant will become the glorious church triumphant.

4

Our Church—
Is It the Remnant Church?

In his recent book Clifford Goldstein, editor of *Liberty* magazine, the voice of the Religious Liberty department of the General Conference, launched into a most detailed listing of examples of the sins within God's church. The picture he presented was alarming, as surely it was meant to be. These were genuine cases. One of Russell's sons was taught by one tragic example cited. We, in our extensive writings outlining a call to righteousness, have never dared to mention that case, nor numerous others which have come to our attention during our many years of denominational service. Even now we dare not provide such a list as we believe it would not serve any noble purpose. Yet sadly, Goldstein's list is just the tip of the iceberg in what has become an amazing departure from the holy life which once characterized the members of the Seventh-day Adventist Church.

Yet, since Clifford Goldstein's list is now public knowledge through its publication by the Pacific Press, we quote what he has asserted.

> A twelve-year-old is repeatedly dragged into bed by her remnant-church father while her remnant-church mom does nothing.
>
> A young woman who has read remnant-church literature comes to Sabbath worship. No one greets her, asks her name, or talks to her—except an elderly saint who sneers at the pearls dangling from her neck.
>
> A child cries. His parents, both leaders in the local remnant church, divorce after years of smiling in public and fighting at home.
>
> A young adult burns with hatred toward the remnant. Her father—head elder, Sabbath school teacher, and Pathfinder leader—beats his wife and then goes out and gives Bible studies.
>
> A remnant-church minister—*minister!*—is arrested for robbing a bank.

A teacher at a remnant-church academy is caught in bed with another man's wife. The enraged husband strangles him.

Some, denouncing the doctrines of the remnant, accuse it of heresy; others, claiming that it has deviated doctrinally, accuse it of apostasy.

A remnant-church member opens his motorcycle dealership on Sabbath.

Parents torture themselves with remorse; after years of sacrificing to send their children to remnant-schools, they see all of them renounce the remnant faith.

Standing before a remnant-church hospital that performs abortions, a Christian holds a sign that says, "Thou shalt not kill."

Vanity Fair runs an article about a southern California doctor arrested for murdering a patient in his office. The magazine states that the doctor had been a pillar of his community and in "the Seventh-day Adventist Church"—the remnant church.*

These sordid clips barely begin to catalog the litany of lies uttered and sins committed by God's "great Advent family," those preparing for translation at Christ's Second Coming. How many members could write a chapter, if not a book, about what has been done by those who cloak themselves, not only under the mantle of Christianity but under the folds of the "remnant church" ? No doubt, Adventist young people could write some of the bitterest, most painful volumes.

As a result, many have been asking, "How can all these sins—incest, adultery, even murder—be in the remnant church?"

Or—is it *really* the remnant church?   (Clifford Goldstein, *The Remnant,* Pacific Press, 1994, pp. 9, 10).

The advertising for this book, *The Remnant,* both on its back cover and in the various North American Union papers states, "Incest, Adultery, Theft, Prejudice, Murder. A description of those who have rejected God in these last days? No, Just a sampling of the sins found in the pews of a church which describes itself as 'the remnant.'"

---

*We ourselves know of at least four other convicted Seventh-day Adventist murderers.

This advertising emphasized the sins of those in the pews. Since in his twelve examples Brother Goldstein has mentioned two pastors, it would have been reasonable to have referred also to the sins found in the pulpit.

Some will no doubt question whether the author was proper in listing such sins, for it is possible that, rather than crying and sighing over these terrible examples of the state of our church, some may rather be titillated by the revelations. All those who bear a ministry of reproof run such a risk.

Others may enquire how a General Conference editor escaped the ire of his colleagues in that office for his presentation of this most unflattering exposure of the state of our church. Still others will question the wisdom of the Pacific Press in publishing this material.

We cannot bring to mind any self-supporting ministry publication which has brought to light such an array of disclosures in the brief space of a book. Yet many self-supporting ministries are accused of being critical and disloyal when reproving far more discretely the sinful trends in God's church. How did this author escape such an evaluation? Why does he retain his post? Not only has he "criticized" lay people, but ministers also.

Perhaps this book escaped an ecclesiastical veto because it discretely mentioned no sins of any denominational administrators. Since this is the most sensitive and powerful element in God's church, many believe that discretion is the better part of valor with regard to pointing out problems among conference, Union, Division and General Conference officers and departmental leaders. Yet Clifford Goldstein could have expanded his list with similar sins discovered in the last ten years among those in such leadership posts. But we believe little would have been achieved for the preservation of God's truth.

We say this, not because we believe that the sole purpose of God's church is to preach truth and ignore the obligation to rebuke soul-destroying error and lowered standards. Many today do believe that the ministry of reproof has no place in God's church. But we do not share this unscriptural position, which only permits Satan's sophistries to permeate the church of God without resistance. Only rank cowardice could promote such a position in

God's church. Yet it is likely that the majority of our pastors and elders and administrators in the western world see little need to oppose the wiles of the devil within our ranks.

But what was the daily work of our Example?

> His [Jesus'] days were passed in ministry to the crowds that pressed upon Him, and in unveiling the treacherous sophistry of the rabbis   (*Thoughts from the Mount of Blessing,* p. 102).

Christ undertook the two primary duties of every believer—to minister to God's blood-bought heritage and to open their eyes to Satanic ploys which are designed to cause such delusion of mind that even earnest souls will be eternally lost. Both ministries are mandatory. Even in this, the era of excused sin, it is the duty of true followers of Christ to

> Cry aloud, spare not, lift up thy voice like a trumpet, and shew my people their transgression, and the house of Jacob their sins   (Isaiah 58:1).

Yet when such a duty is faithfully performed, it is strenuously resented. As in Christ's day, the prime movers against the message of reform are frequently found to be church administrators who utilize the media avenues of the church to incite the anger of the laity against faithful ministers and laymen who are represented as "causing division, disloyalty to God's church and being critical of leadership." Such were the accusations against our Example.

> But in order to maintain their own power, these leaders determined to break down the influence of Jesus. His arraignment before the Sanhedrin, and an open condemnation of His teachings, would aid in effecting this; for the people still had great reverence for their religious leaders. Whoever dared to condemn the rabbinical requirements, or attempt to lighten the burdens they had brought upon the people, was regarded as guilty, not only of blasphemy, but of treason. On this ground the rabbis hoped to excite suspicion of Christ. They represented Him as trying to overthrow the established customs, thus *causing* division among the people. . .
>
>   (*The Desire of Ages,* p. 205 emphasis added).

As in Christ's day, so today,

> If the priests [ministers] and rabbis [theologians] had not interposed, His [Christ's] teaching would have wrought such a reformation as this world has never witnessed
> *(The Desire of Ages,* p. 205).

How crucial it is for the remnant church to learn the lessons of the past!

Of course it is possible to point out the sins of God's people in the spirit of vindictiveness and even exhilaration. But such only performs the work of the evil one. If a desire for the eternal salvation of our brethren and sisters and the uplifting of our Lord is not our motivation, then we best serve in following a course of silence.

Many, when the ministry of reproof by the Biblical prophets is cited as a precedent for their own course, arrogantly retort, "So you think that you are a prophet, do you?" Such a rhetorical question is as improper as it is spiteful. It affords no honor to the one who poses the question. We are told by God's servant precisely what *our* work is.

> What is our work? The same as that given to John the Baptist
> *(Testimonies to the Church,* vol. 8, p. 9).

Then what was John the Baptist's work?

> He [John the Baptist] was to bear to the world an unflinching testimony in reproving and denouncing sin
> *(Selected Messages,* book 2, p. 147).

Even more telling,

> In his mission the Baptist had stood as a fearless reprover of iniquity, both in high places and in low
> *(The Desire of Ages,* p. 215).

God's servant, after signaling our work as identical with that of John the Baptist, informed us that,

> All who are truly engaged in the work of the Lord for these last days will have a decided message to bear
> *(Testimonies to the Church,* vol. 8, p. 9).

Since the bulk of apostasy promoted in God's remnant church emanates from our theologians, and since there is an alarming reluctance of church administrators to openly expose such apostasy and to cleanse our colleges and universities at their source, there is a sense of defensiveness when faithful men accept the burden which should be shouldered by those men. This defensiveness exposes itself in attack and punitive actions against those who do perform their god-ordained duty in this respect.

As we write this volume during the closing days of 1994, the 1994 Annual Council has considered a massive thirty-six alterations to the *Church Manual*. When the South Pacific *Record* (November 5, 1994) reported this fact, it cited but four of the proposed alterations, three of which were related to church discipline. These proposed alterations will not follow more closely the counsels of inspiration concerning the matter of dealing with apostasy and breaches of the decalogue; rather they will be used to tighten measures against those who sincerely proclaim the need for a mighty reform in God's church within the ranks of administrators, ministers and laity. These reformers, as in the case of Clifford Goldstein, would no doubt escape the penalties to be enforced if they did not call for our conference and other presidents and officers to break their unaccountable silence in the face of shameful apostasy and standards worldwide and to cease their persistent denunciations of those presenting the Elijah message, which is the straight testimony of the True Witness to the church of Laodicea. It is time that such leaders who choose to improperly use power to prevent reform, recognize that their work has long been predicted.

> I asked the meaning of the shaking I had seen and was shown that it would be caused by the straight testimony called forth by the counsel of the True Witness to the Laodiceans. This will have its effect upon the heart of the receiver, and will lead him to exalt the standard and pour forth the straight truth. Some will not bear this straight testimony. They will rise up against it, and this is what will cause a shaking among God's people (*Early Writings*, p. 270).

It is a fearful matter to be part of that group fulfilling this prophecy. We plead with our leaders in God's remnant church to consider their responsibility in this matter. Our plea is not based upon any other motive than a desire for their redemption and for the salvation of souls led astray by their fierce opposition to truth and to those who present it.

Even some who stand for truth have a faulted view of their responsibility to guard the one object of Christ's supreme regard. Such must carefully read Inspiration. It is clear and powerful. Two examples are cited.

> It is not enough to merely profess to believe the truth. All the soldiers of the cross of Christ virtually obligate themselves to enter the crusade against the adversary of souls, to condemn wrong and sustain righteousness. But the message of the True Witness reveals the fact that a terrible deception is upon our people, which makes it necessary to come to them with warnings, to break their spiritual slumber, and arouse them to decided action   (*Testimonies to the Church,* vol. 3, p. 254).

The second statement is even more pointed.

> The church is Christ's fortress in a revolted world, and it must be strictly guarded against the enemy's wily arts. In it no laws are to be acknowledged but the laws of God. Those whom God has set as watchmen are not to look on quietly while efforts are being made to lead men and women away from the truth into false paths. Careful watch is to be kept against seducing spirits and doctrines of devils. God calls upon ministers and medical missionaries to take a firm stand for the right. The severe denunciations that Christ uttered against the Pharisees for teaching for doctrine the commandments of men show the necessity for guarding against all theories that are not in harmony with the truth of God's word
> (*Medical Ministry,* pp. 89, 90).

Surely, after the publication of such a litany of evil within God's church by Clifford Goldstein and the Pacific Press, no fair-minded Seventh-day Adventist will ever again accept the condemnation by church leaders of faithful pastors and laymen claiming these earnest workers are critical of the church when they call for much-needed reform in far less specific terms.

With Clifford Goldstein's documentation of the vileness within God's remnant church, is it *really* the remnant church? Strangely, the answer of Inspiration is in the affirmative.

> I saw that the remnant were not prepared for what is coming upon the earth. Stupidity, like lethargy, seemed to hang upon the minds of most of those who profess to believe that we are having the last message (*Early Writings*, p. 119).

Thus stupidity and lethargy was seen to characterize the remnant church.

But let each of us be warned: ever so shortly the probation for God's church will close, and then His church triumphant will possess only those whom Christ has purified.

> But who may abide the day of his coming? and who shall stand when he appeareth? for he is like a refiner's fire, and like fullers' soap: and he shall sit as a refiner and purifier of silver: and he shall purify the sons of Levi, and purge them as gold and silver, that they may offer unto the Lord an offering in righteousness. Then shall the offering of Judah and Jerusalem be pleasant unto the Lord, as in the days of old, and as in former years (Malachi 3:2-4).

But before that day God has called His faithful messengers to do a work of reform.

> Behold, I will send my messenger, and he shall prepare the way before me: and the Lord, whom ye seek, shall suddenly come to his temple, even the messenger of the covenant, whom ye delight in: behold, he shall come, saith the Lord of hosts (Malachi 3:1).

Woe to those who do not heed those messengers, and who do all in their power to deflect the messages and to press God's people into an even deeper coma than they are presently experiencing.

We cite as an instance of this, an undated letter written by the secretary of the South Pacific Division to every senior elder in Australia and New Zealand, and posted in October 1994. The letter is quoted in full, omitting only the final greetings.

> Earlier this year a book written by Doctor Roy Adams entitled *The Nature of Christ* was released onto the market. Doctor Adams is currently connected with the staff of the Ministerial Association at the General Conference. Over the years the Nature of Christ has become the focus of much discussion and

debate and this book, written in an easy to read manner, deals with the various issues and aspects relating to this important subject.

Because of the significance of this doctrine, particularly as it relates to some aspects of our eschatology, the South Pacific Division has voted to distribute one copy of this book free to every senior elder in Australia and New Zealand. Enclosed you will find this copy which comes with our compliments and sincere prayer that you will find the book to be both challenging and edifying.

We would also like to suggest that when you have read the book you pass it on to your fellow elders for them to read, and then, if you do have a church library, perhaps it can be placed in there as there could be some other church members who may also be interested in reading it.

While writing we would also like to take this opportunity to thank you each one individually for your valued ministry and loyalty. We recognize that it is not always easy serving as a senior elder and "guardian of the flock" in these difficult times when there is so much dissension, lethargy and criticism by various groups and individuals who seem bent on undermining people's confidence in God's Church and its leadership. However, we believe the Lord has called you to your important responsibility in the church where you serve and "who knoweth whether thou art come to the Kingdom for such a time as this."

Since the book, *The Nature of Christ,* Review and Herald, 1994, denies that which inspiration clearly teaches, it can only lull our people into a perilous slumber. That book absolutely denies the clearest teaching of Hebrews 4:15.

> For we have not an high priest which cannot be touched with the feeling of our infirmities; but was in all points tempted like as we are, yet without sin   (Hebrews 4:15).

According to Scripture, Christ was "in all points tempted like as we are, yet without sin" (Heb. 4:15). What does this mean?

"The translation in the King James Version really does not do justice to the Greek," an Adventist New Testament scholar said to me recently. "*Kata panta,* the expression used in the passage, is extremely difficult to convert to English."

"But we have to translate it," I pressed him.

"Well, that's why we have people study Greek—so that they don't have to translate it. But the best we've been able to come up with is that Jesus was tempted '*variously and intensively,*' an expression that (given the person Christ was) emphasizes the rigor and intensity of the temptations He had to endure."

That makes sense to me, but I suspect that such a radical departure from the usual translation might be too much for many readers. So allow me to deal with the issue on the basis of the familiar translation in the King James Version: He "was in all points tempted like as we are."

Does this mean that Christ experienced every single specific temptation that I face? I don't think so. There are factors that render a specific temptation different—not unique, but different.

For example, temptations are sometimes related to *time.* The temptation to hold slaves or to be a pirate is not generally as strong today as it once was. And I rather doubt that Jesus was bothered by either.

Then there is the question of *place.* The specific temptations that confront a person living in metropolitan Manila, London, or New York today could hardly be the same as those that faced Christ in the small, rural village of Nazareth in the first century. Not that Nazareth was a paradise, of course. Remember that some wondered whether any good thing could come from there (John 1:46). But the anonymity afforded by the huge metropolises of today was completely unknown in Christ's time.

Then, third, there is the question of *personality and life setting.* Christ could not have had the particular temptations of a woman, for example. He never had to face the issue of aborting a fetus. Christ was never a human father, had never been married, and, therefore, did not meet the particular temptations of a father—with teenagers, say. Or of a husband or

wife having to live with a difficult or impossible spouse
(Roy Adams, *The Nature of Christ,* Review & Herald, 1974, pp 74–76).

Unfortunately, theologians have a habit of rationalizing away the clearest statements of inspiration.

Further, the Division secretary's letter is designed to rally the elders to oppose those who humbly take their stand for truth and declare error to be just what it is. Many in Australia and New Zealand wonder when their division leadership last upheld sound doctrine both by condemning error and promoting truth.

Each one of us dare not risk the ire of the flock, much less the ire of God.

> The people turned upon their ministers with bitter hate and reproached them, saying, "You have not warned us. You told us that all the world was to be converted, and cried, Peace, peace, to quiet every fear that was aroused. You have not told us of this hour; and those who warned us of it you declared to be fanatics and evil men, who would ruin us." But I saw that the ministers did not escape the wrath of God. Their suffering was tenfold greater than that of their people
> *(Early Writings,* p. 282).

Let God's people listen to the voice of reform, let each of us count the cost of silence and the price to be paid for the promotion of error in this time of vile apostasy within God's church. Let us strive, under God's grace, to be among those who are God's true remnant "not having spot or wrinkle or any such thing" and those who are "holy and without blemish." (Ephesians 5:27)

5

The True Remnant

The concept of the remnant is of central importance to our understanding of the church. Frequently the Spirit of Prophecy refers to the Seventh-day Adventist Church as the remnant church. This has led many superficial students to believe that those in the Seventh-day Adventist Church are the remnant, and the rest of the world is outside the fellowship of Christ. However, this concept cannot be sustained in a careful study of Inspiration.

The Word of God refers to the remnant as the remnant of Israel (Zephaniah 3:13), or the remnant of the woman (church) (Rev. 12:17). Thus in a very specific way, at the end of time, these prophecies of the remnant must be applied to those who have had greatest light and have had greatest privileges and opportunities to ready themselves for the coming of Jesus Christ. The very small remnant (Isaiah 1:9) will thus be drawn from the faithful who have possessed this great light, privileges, and opportunities and have made a high profession of faith. An examination of both Old and New Testaments makes it plain that only a small number of those who are in God's church are truly part of His people, and will be provided an entrance into God's eternal home. This is a realization of great seriousness. It presents to the true believer cause for great self examination and earnest submission of his or her life to the King of kings. It is not the Seventh-day Adventist Church that will be delivered. It is the remnant of the Seventh-day Adventist Church.

> And it shall come to pass, that whosoever shall call on the name of the LORD shall be delivered: for in mount Zion and in Jerusalem shall be deliverance, as the LORD hath said, and in the remnant whom the LORD shall call (Joel 2:32).

Now there are essential lessons to learn from this text. This passage specifically focuses upon the final deliverance of God's people. God first clarifies the fact that the deliverance does not come outside of His church; for deliverance will take place in Mount Zion and in Jerusalem. Frequently the servant of the Lord refers to the Seventh-day Adventist Church as modern Israel. Again, sometimes Sister White implies that Israel consists of faithful believers and at other times she includes the unfaithful in Israel.

> Those who hunger and thirst after righteousness were to be numbered among the Israel of God
> *(Prophets and Kings, p.371).*

> For forty years did unbelief, murmuring, and rebellion shut out ancient Israel from the land of Canaan. The same sins have delayed the entrance of modern Israel into the heavenly Canaan *(Selected Messages, vol. 1, p.69).*

> I was shown that those who are trying to obey God and purify their souls through obedience to the truth are God's chosen people, His modern Israel *(Testimonies, vol 2, p.109).*

> We are numbered with Israel. All the instruction given to the Israelites of old concerning the education and training of their children, all the promises of blessing through obedience, are for us *(Ministry of Healing, p.405).*

There is no way that a voluntary separation from the Seventh-day Adventist Church can be sustained from scripture. The book of Joel contains an end-time message, a message that has far greater relevance for those of us living in the final moment of earth's history than for those who lived in the day in which this book was written.

Again, it is demonstrated from this book that only the remnant will be saved, for only the remnant have forged an unbreakable relationship with their God. Perhaps the most remarkable chapter in all the Bible concerning the remnant is Isaiah 11. This chapter deals with the deliverance of the remnant by the branch of Jesse.

> And there shall come forth a rod out of the stem of Jesse, and a Branch shall grow out of his roots (Isaiah 11:1).

Revelation 5:5 leaves no doubt that this root is Jesus.

> And one of the elders saith unto me, Weep not: behold, the Lion of the tribe of Juda, the Root of David, hath prevailed to open the book, and to loose the seven seals thereof
> (Revelation 5:5).

The True Remnant

Paul recognized Isaiah's message described the reign of Jesus.

> And again, Esaias saith, there shall be a root of Jesse, and he that shall rise to reign over the Gentiles; in him shall the Gentiles trust (Romans 15:12).

This prophecy of Isaiah has been wonderfully fulfilled as millions of Gentiles have accepted Jesus as their Redeemer. That Isaiah is dealing with the judgment time is perfectly plain.

> And [the spirit of the Lord, resting upon the stem of Jesse] shall make him of quick understanding in the fear of the LORD: and he shall not judge after the sight of his eyes, neither reprove after the hearing of his ears: but with righteousness shall he judge the poor, and reprove with equity for the meek of the earth: and he shall smite the earth with the rod of his mouth, and with the breath of his lips shall he slay the wicked (Isaiah 11:3, 4).

Thus in the context of the judgment we have this promise,

> And it shall come to pass in that day, that the Lord shall set his hand again the second time to recover the remnant of his people (Isaiah 11:11).

The remnant is also referred to as the elect (Matthew 24:24; Isaiah 45:4; 65:9, 22; Matthew 24:22; Mark 13:20; Matthew 24:31; Mark 13:27) and the saints (Revelation 14:12; 1 Corinthians 6:2; Revelation 5:8). Frequently in the Bible and in the Spirit of Prophecy the term "saints" is used to designate those preparing for the return of Jesus Christ. Clear evidence is given of the application of the Old Testament remnant prophecies to the end-time by Paul in his letter to the Romans.

> Esaias also crieth concerning Israel, Though the number of the children of Israel be as the sand of the sea, a remnant shall be saved: for he will finish the work, and cut it short in righteousness: because a short work will the Lord make upon the earth. As Esaias said before, Except the Lord of Sabbaoth had left us a seed, we had been as Sodoma, and been made like unto Gomorrha (Romans 9:27–29).

In this passage Paul quotes from three prophecies of the book of Isaiah (Isaiah 10:22, 23; 1:9).

Of special importance to us as we understand the remnant is the early reference of the prophet Isaiah.

> Except the Lord of hosts had left unto us a very small remnant, we should have been as Sodom, and we should have been like unto Gomorrah (Isaiah 1:9).

History attests that never have more than a remnant of God's people been faithful to Him. But it is because of this small, faithful, loyal remnant that God's people have been repeatedly spared. Yet the faithful have always been despised, rejected, and persecuted by the majority apostates, who are wholly unaware that their prosperity and even their existence hinges upon the loyalty of the very remnant they despise. So precious is the remnant to God that He promised Abraham that He would not destroy Sodom and Gomorrah if there were ten just men in those cities. (Genesis 18:32) Thus it was in the days of Isaiah that though apostasy was rampant, God preserved His people because of the faithfulness of the remnant. So it is today that our church has been spared the judgments of God because of the faithfulness of a very small remnant. This is not idle speculation, because Paul has taken this very prophecy of Isaiah and, as we have seen in Romans 9:27, applied it to the end of time.

Jesus confirmed that few will be saved in His kingdom.

> Because strait is the gate, and narrow is the way, which leadeth unto life, and few there be that find it (Matthew 7:14).

Realizing these facts, it is a tragic acknowledgement that the vast majority of those who are members of the Seventh-day Adventist Church will not be ready for the kingdom of heaven. Those who have had the greatest light, who have had such wonderful opportunities, will in large proportions fail of eternal life. With great agony of heart and burden of soul, we seek to reach out to the members of modern Israel, urging them to take hold of the great principles of truth and righteousness, and to ready themselves for the coming of Jesus Christ. Surely in the most pleading way the Lord is saying,

> As I live. . . I have no pleasure in the death of the wicked; but that the wicked turn from his way and live: turn ye, turn ye from your evil ways; for why will ye die, O house of Israel?
> (Ezekiel 33:11).

Can such a plea fall on deaf ears among the membership of the Seventh-day Adventist Church? Tragically, it is doing so today. Such a plea to our fellow church members ought to be received with the greatest earnestness by every true Seventh-day Adventist, for the greatest disappointment will be to those who had every opportunity, but fail of eternal life.

Who are the remnant who will inherit eternal life? The Bible leaves us in no doubt.

> The remnant of Israel shall not do iniquity, nor speak lies; neither shall a deceitful tongue be found in their mouth: for they shall feed and lie down, and none shall make them afraid
> (Zephaniah 3:13).

Is it any wonder that Satan is spreading, as a prairie fire, the concept of "sin and live" ; the concept that God's people will continue to sin until Jesus comes. But a look at the reverse side of this text demonstrates that the majority of Israel do iniquity, and as such will be lost from the kingdom of heaven. Such a tragic conclusion is drawn also from the New Testament.

> And the dragon was wroth with the woman, and went to make war with the remnant of her seed, which keep the commandments of God, and have the testimony of Jesus Christ
> (Revelation 12:17).

Recognizing that the dragon is Satan (Revelation 12:9), that the woman is the church (Revelation 12:1), and that the testimony of Jesus Christ is the Spirit of Prophecy (Revelation 19:10), then we understand that this text can properly be rendered, "And Satan was wroth with the church, and went to make war with the remnant of her seed, which keep the commandments of God and have the Spirit of Prophecy."

It is a most sobering thought to realize that Satan is not making war upon the whole of the Seventh-day Adventist Church. Indeed, his war is only against the remnant. The reason is obvious. Those who profess to be God's true, faithful people, but who are living a life of pretence and indifference, are Satan's premium ambassadors. He has no reason to make war against them. The remnant keep the commandments of God and have the Spirit of Prophecy. This text leads to the conclusion that the majority of Seventh-day Adventists do not keep the commandments of God and they have little regard for the messages of the Spirit of Prophecy.

That is why there is such overwhelming apostasy, indifference, worldliness, transgression and carelessness in the ranks of the professed followers of Jesus Christ. No wonder the Revelator says that we are:

> Wretched, and miserable, and poor, and blind, and naked
> (Revelation 3:17).

Unfortunately, not only are many members of the Seventh-day Adventist Church blissfully living in carnal security, believing that they are heaven bound, but there are those, even in high ecclesiastical position, who are encouraging a carnal security among the ranks of those who have no right of assurance because they have not followed the true principles of God. There have been those who have emphasized the great "multitude which no man could number" (Revelation 7:9) to propose that large numbers will be saved from the Seventh-day Adventist Church (see Week of Prayer reading, second Sabbath 1993) but such will lead only to reinforce those living in a false carnal security. Inspiration does not equivocate.

> To obey the commandments of God is the only way to obtain His favor (*Testimonies*, vol. 4, p.28).

> Let none imagine that without earnest effort on their part they can obtain the assurance of God's love
> (*Messages to Young People*, p.113).

> In the full assurance of his faith the aged disciple exhorted his brethren to steadfastness of purpose in the Christian life. "Give diligence" he pleaded, "to make your calling and election sure: for if ye do these things, ye shall never fall: for so an entrance shall be ministered unto you abundantly into the everlasting kingdom of our Lord and Saviour Jesus Christ."

Precious assurance! Glorious is the hope before the believer as he advances by faith toward the heights of Christian perfection! *(Acts of the Apostles,* p.533).

We cannot have the assurance and perfect confiding trust in Christ as our Saviour until we acknowledge Him as our King and are obedient to His commandments
(Faith and Works, p.16).

Those who are longing for the return of Jesus while unsurrendered to Jesus face terrible consequences in the judgment.

Not every one that saith unto me, Lord, Lord, shall enter into the kingdom of heaven; but he that doeth the will of my Father which is in heaven. Many will say to me in that day, Lord, Lord, have we not prophesied in thy name? and in thy name have cast out devils? and in thy name done many wonderful works? And then will I profess unto them, I never knew you: depart from me, ye that work iniquity
(Matthew 7:21–23).

Myriads of professed believers will come to the end of earth's probation without the oil of the Holy Spirit in their lamp, and therefore will be lost eternally. Little did they realize how far they were from the kingdom of heaven, and they are lost while believing that they were saved.

In the concept of the church, these people claim to be part of the remnant church. Their membership, no doubt, is retained upon the membership books of earth, but they are far from the kingdom. God has done everything to woo them to His kingdom, but they have been lost because of their own indifference and choices. Heaven is within their reach but their souls are far from the perfect Pattern.

The class represented by the foolish virgins are not hypocrites. They have a regard for the truth, they have advocated the truth, they are attracted to those who believe the truth; but they have not yielded themselves to the Holy Spirit's working. They have not fallen upon the Rock, Christ Jesus, and permitted their old nature to be broken up
(Christ's Object Lessons, p.411).

6

The Flock and the Fold

It is only to be expected that in the pastoral society that dominated Judah, many examples of God's dealing with His people were cast in pastoral terms. The sheep fold was a symbol of protection as each night the shepherd brought the sheep into the fold to secure their safety against predators. Thus the Lord, in illustrating the chosen agency for the spiritual protection of His people, refers to His church as the fold of His sheep. While not specifically identifying God's people as His flock, nevertheless Sister White captures the concept of God's desire to protect His flock from Satanic intrusion.

> Consider, my brethren and sisters, that the Lord has a people, a chosen people, His church, to be His own, His own fortress, which He holds in a sin-stricken, revolted world; and He intends that no authority should be known in it, no laws be acknowledged by it, but His own
> *(Testimonies to Ministers,* p.15–16).

> The church is Christ's fortress in a revolted world, and it must be strictly guarded against the enemy's wily arts. In it no laws are to be acknowledged but the laws of God. Those whom God has set as watchmen are not to look on quietly while efforts are being made to lead men and women away from the truth into false paths. Careful watch is to be kept against seducing spirits and doctrines of devils. God calls upon ministers and medical missionaries to take a firm stand for the right. The severe denunciations that Christ uttered against the Pharisees for teaching for doctrine the commandments of men show the necessity for guarding against all theories that are not in harmony with the truth of God's word
> *(Medical Ministry,* p.89, 90).

If these counsels were followed, the fold of God, His church would be an invincible fortress against all the seductive deceptions of Satan. God's people would be protected against the sophistries of the evil one, and the church, both individually and corporately would reflect the glory of God and would be united in truth and righteousness. But even the most optimistic among us cannot see the present Seventh-day Adventist church in this light. God has put a hedge about His people.

> He has built a hedge—the Ten Commandments—about His subjects to preserve them from the results of transgression
> *(Counsels to Parents, Teachers, and Students,* p.454).

> To this people were committed the oracles of God. They were hedged about by the precepts of His law, the everlasting principles of truth, justice, and purity. Obedience to these principles was to be their protection, for it would save them from destroying themselves by sinful practices. And as the tower in the vineyard, God placed in the midst of the land His holy temple *(Christ's Object Lessons,* p.287, 288).

Just as in olden times such a protection was placed around God's people, so it is today.

> So far from making arbitrary requirements, God's law is given to men as a hedge, a shield. Whoever accepts its principle is preserved from evil. Fidelity to God involves fidelity to man. Thus the law guards the rights, the individuality, of every human being. It restrains the superior from oppression, and the subordinate from disobedience. It insures man's well-being, both for this world and for the world to come. To the obedient, it is the pledge of eternal life, for it expresses the principles that endure forever *(Education,* p.76, 77).

But when the law of God is breached, the fold becomes defective and the hedge vulnerable, and Satan is able to prey upon God's flock, seeking to destroy and corrupt. The Seventh-day Adventist church is God's fold in these end times.

> The church on earth is greatly beloved by God. It is the fold provided for the sheep of His pasture
> *(Signs of the Times,* October 31, 1900).

Yet the servant of the Lord sees terrible defects in His fold. Thus she goes on to say,

> But the Lord will not serve with the sins of His people. Many times He has suffered calamity and defeat to come upon them because they have glorified themselves, weaving false prin-

ciples into their practice. He willingly forgives those who repent, but He will remove His favor from those who go on sinning, exalting self, and mingling the sacred with the common. Terrible judgments will destroy those who have misrepresented Him, saying, "The temple of the Lord, the temple of the Lord, the temple of the Lord, are these," when their example is misleading (Ibid.).

God has provided His church, His Seventh-day Adventist Church, as a protective fold for the sheep of His pasture. Nevertheless, God realizes that His fold would contain many unfaithful sheep, and eventually He will cast them out of the fold. There have been many who have confused the fold with the flock. The fold is the church, the flock is the sheep of the church. In both the books of Jeremiah and Ezekiel, God reveals that faithful sheep will be driven out of His fold by unfaithful pastors. This happens before God sifts the unfaithful out of His fold.

> Woe be unto the pastors that destroy and scatter the sheep of my pasture! saith the Lord. Therefore thus saith the Lord God of Israel against the pastors that feed my people; Ye have scattered my flock, and driven them away, and have not visited them: behold, I will visit upon you the evil of your doings, saith the Lord. And I will gather the remnant of my flock out of all countries whither I have driven them, and will bring them again to their folds; and they shall be fruitful and increase. And I will set up shepherds over them which shall feed them: and they shall fear no more, nor be dismayed, neither shall they be lacking, saith the Lord
> (Jeremiah 23:1–4).

For thus saith the Lord God; Behold, I, even I, will both search my sheep, and seek them out. As a shepherd seeketh out his flock in the day that he is among his sheep that are scattered; so will I seek out my sheep, and will deliver them out of all places where they have been scattered in the cloudy and dark day. And I will bring them out from the people, and gather them from the countries, and will bring them to their own land, and feed them upon the mountains of Israel by the rivers, and in all the inhabited places of the country. I will feed them in a good pasture, and upon the high mountains of

Israel shall their fold be: there shall they lie in a good fold, and in a fat pasture shall they feed upon the mountains of Israel (Ezekiel 34:11–14).

At the time the wicked are shaken out of the church, God has promised to bring the faithful scattered from the flock back to their fold.

And I will gather the remnant of my flock out of all countries whither I have driven them, and will bring them again to their folds; and they shall be fruitful and increase
(Jeremiah 23:3).

There are those who have wrongly concluded that the fold is the people, the faithful people; but that cannot be sustained by the Word of God. It is the flock that represents the people. These have been scattered abroad. It is sobering to note, however, that it is only the remnant of that flock that are brought back into His fold at the end of time. This is confirmed by the prophets, Ezekiel and Micah.

I will feed them in a good pasture, and upon the high mountains of Israel shall their fold be: there shall they lie in a good fold, and in a fat pasture shall they feed upon the mountains of Israel (Ezekiel 34:14).

I will surely assemble, O Jacob, all of thee; I will surely gather the remnant of Israel; I will put them together as the sheep of Bozrah, as the flock in the midst of their fold: they shall make great noise by reason of the multitude of men
(Micah 2:12).

When the faithful flock is brought back to its fold there will be great rejoicing as the Spirit of God reunites, in one unbroken family, His faithful people who have wavered neither to the left, nor to the right from the great truths of God. This is the time of which Jesus spake when He said:

They shall put you out of the synagogues: yea, the time cometh, that whosoever killeth you will think that he doeth God service (John 16:2).

God has never lost sight of His faithful flock, nor has He been unmindful of the difficulties that they have had to face. It is at this time that the prophecy of the Psalmist will be fulfilled:

> So we thy people and sheep of thy pasture will give thee thanks for ever: we will shew forth thy praise to all generations (Psalms 79:13).

What a thrilling time this is going to be! We pray that all members of the Seventh-day Adventist Church will realize how much God loves His flock, and that they will respond to His call.

> Know ye that the Lord he is God: it is he that hath made us, and not we ourselves; we are his people, and the sheep of his pasture (Psalm 100:3).

> For he is our God; and we are the people of his pasture, and the sheep of his hand. To day if ye will hear his voice, harden not your heart, as in the provocation, and as in the day of temptation in the wilderness (Psalm 95:7, 8).

Some become discouraged when trials and persecutions come to them. Some wonder if God has forsaken them, or deserted them, but God is ever with us, He will never leave us nor forsake us. In the most tender language, Isaiah expresses his absolute confidence in the leading of God.

> He shall feed his flock like a shepherd: he shall gather the lambs with his arm, and carry them in his bosom, and shall gently lead those that are with young (Isaiah 40:11).

The flock will be fed, and they shall find their folds.

> I will feed my flock, and I will cause them to lie down, saith the Lord God (Ezekiel 34:15).

It does not matter from which perspective we look at the issue of the flock, God has given us the clearest indication that He will bring it back to His fold, the Seventh-day Adventist Church. This is accomplished just prior to the close of probationary time, no doubt at the time of the completion of the shaking of His church.

7

The Wheat and the Tares

The Word of God gives us instruction concerning the state of the church just prior to the close of probation in the parable of the tares. In the book, *Christ's Object Lessons,* Sister White entitles the relevant chapter simply, "Tares." This, of course, does not diminish the wonderful statements about the faithful wheat, but nevertheless the parable's emphasis is upon the tares.

From Matthew's account we can clearly define the following:

1. It is because of the sleepiness of God's workers that tares come into the church (Matt. 13:25). This surely is consistent with the Laodicean message and the message of the wise and foolish virgins. Had God's workers been awake, Satan could never have sown the tares in the remnant church. In this sense we all stand culpable.

Over two decades ago, while he was serving as president of West Indies College in Jamaica, Colin met two men who were passing through. They claimed that there should be no conditions upon which a person is accepted into the membership of God's church. They urged that anyone who desired to be members should be allowed into church fellowship even if they be smokers or drinkers or adulterers for it was *their* choices whether or not to join the Seventh-day Adventist Church. They declared they belonged to a church which could not be touched by the Conference. On inquiry, they told Colin that they were members of the Burbank Church in the Southern California conference. Indeed, they were wrong, for that church was disbanded over such outright apostasy just a few years later, and then was reorganized, and so it should have been. Obviously, if we knowingly allow unconverted people to enter into God's remnant church, we are aiding and abetting the work of Satan. Soon such unconverted people would become a majority in the church and Satan's, not God's, decision would be made. There is powerful evidence that such has already taken place in many contemporary churches.

2. We know that the tares are sown by Satan (Matt. 13:39). The servant of the Lord expresses plainly that

> While the Lord brings into the church those who are truly converted, Satan at the same time brings persons who are not converted into its fellowship (*The Faith I Live By,* p.305).

It does not take much consideration to discover why Satan brings members into the Seventh-day Adventist Church. Satan has a desire to sabotage the Seventh-day Adventist Church. When one is fighting an enemy from without, it is much easier to focus the attack and the defense; but when saboteurs and traitors are within the camp, it is well nigh impossible to defend adequately against such subterfuge.

Satan's most direct attack is against the youth of the church. Peter, in directing his counsel to the younger members of the church recommended them to

> Be sober, be vigilant; because your adversary the devil, as a roaring lion, walketh about, seeking whom he may devour
> (1 Peter 5:8).

John adds a similar thought,

> Woe to the inhabiters of the earth and of the sea ! for the devil is come down unto you, having great wrath, because he knoweth that he hath but a short time (Revelation 12:12).

3. We know that the tares are members of God's remnant church. The Bible says,

> The field is the world; the good seed are the children of the kingdom; but the tares are the children of the wicked one
> (Matthew 13:38).

In commenting upon the Bible statement that the field is "the world," the servant of the Lord says,

> But we must understand this as signifying the church of Christ in the world. The parable is a description of that which pertains to the kingdom of God, His work for the salvation of men; and this work is accomplished through the church. True, the Holy Spirit is gone out into all the world; everywhere it is

moving upon the hearts of men; but it is in the church that we are to grow and ripen for the garner of God
(*Christ's Object Lessons,* p.70).

Thus, until the tares are separated from the wheat, we cannot have a perfect church. That perfect church will appear only as the tares have been gathered in bundles to be burned, and that happens right at the end of probationary time.

4. We know that until the "fruit" had appeared it was almost impossible to tell the difference between the wheat and the tares.

> But when the blade was sprung up, and brought forth fruit, then appeared the tares also (Matt. 13:26).

In commenting upon this, the servant of the Lord says,

> The tares closely resembled the wheat while the blades were green; but when the field was white for the harvest, the worthless weeds bore no likeness to the wheat that bowed under the weight of its full, ripe heads (*Christ's Object Lessons,* p.74).

Now some have been confused on this point. There are those who say we cannot tell the difference between the tares and wheat. Some contend that the tares are not in open sin. But the servant of the Lord clearly identifies the tares as weeds in the above quotation. We have now come to the end of time and the contrast between the wheat and the tares becomes increasingly apparent. Compare Sister White's statement above with the following statement:

> Christ has plainly taught that those who persist in open sin must be separated from the church; but He has not committed to us the work of judging character and motive. He knows our nature too well to entrust this work to us. Should we try to uproot from the church those whom we suppose to be spurious Christians, we should be sure to make mistakes. Often we regard as hopeless subjects the very ones whom Christ is drawing to Himself. Were we to deal with these souls according to our imperfect judgment, it would perhaps extinguish their last hope. Many who think themselves Christians will at last be found wanting. Many will be in heaven who their neighbors supposed would never enter there. Man judges from

appearance, but God judges the heart. The tares and the wheat are to grow together until the harvest; and the harvest is the end of probationary time (*Christ's Object Lessons,* p.71, 72).

What is the meaning of these two statements? Clearly those who are in open violation of God's law should be removed from the fellowship of God's church. This would include adulterers, thieves, and overt Sabbath breakers.

Now the tares are a form of weed that far more closely resemble the wheat than many other weeds, and so these obvious sins will not be seen amongst them. That is why they cannot be removed from the church. However, as we come to the end of time, their worldliness, their indifference, their casualness about their religion becomes increasingly obvious. Religion has become a form, and though they may not be guilty of the worst forms of law breaking, clearly they have a lifestyle wholly inconsistent with those who are preparing for the kingdom of heaven. We believe that we have reached this stage, where, in most cases, the tares are now being clearly revealed.

These tares have no urgency for the time in which we live. They have no burden for their own souls and certainly not for the souls of others. They may be faithful in returning their tithes and give token offerings; they may hold office in their church, but their heart is yet carnal, and their lives do not speak of the fact that Jesus is soon to lay down the censer and return to this earth.

Many in God's church are "playing religion," and the deep, earnest pleadings of the Holy Spirit are ignored. We must realize that the wheat and tares grow together until the harvest, and the harvest is the end of probationary time. It is impossible for us to understand how people reading inspired counsel can believe that God's church at this time contains only faithful members and those who, in every outward respect appear to be faithful Christians. The tares who now bear no resemblance to the wheat will remain in the church until the close of probation.

5. The parable clearly teaches that those in open sin should be removed from the church.

> Christ has plainly taught that those who persist in open sin must be separated from the church (Ibid, p.71).

Unfortunately, in many churches we witness a false concept of love which in reality is indulgence and irresponsibility. Such false love leads many of those who are known to be living in open sin, including adultery, fornication, homosexuality, and theft, to retain their membership within the Seventh-day Adventist Church. What an abomination! Is it any wonder that our church is suffering from such terrible impotence? We are reminded that the secret sin of one man, Achan, led to terrible impotency in the Israel of old. Let us note how the servant of the Lord applies this ancient experience to the modern day church.

> If the presence of one Achan was sufficient to weaken the whole camp of Israel, can we be surprised at the little success which attends our efforts when every church and almost every family has its Achan? (*Testimonies*, vol. 5, p. 157)

The impotency of churches in the Western world is plain for all to see. Surely much of this impotency is due to the sinful negligence of local church leaders who do not have the courage, nor the burden to have their churches fitly represent the Son of God. Leaders pretend that they are showing love and forbearance, when indeed, like Aaron of old, they are showing their weakness and indulgence.

So polluted have our churches become that a General Conference editor was impelled to state in a book published by the Pacific Press, "Incest, adultery, theft, prejudice, murder . . . just a sampling of the sins found in the pews of a church that describes itself as the remnant" (Clifford Goldstein, *The Remnant,* back cover). The same could equally be stated, with the matter of murder excepted, as being samples of sins of those occupying the pulpits in God's remnant church. Thus do the tares flourish in a church which tolerates and even sometimes encourages sin amongst its members.

It has ever been a characteristic of apostasy that members of the church who are steeped in sin are more and more readily overlooked and remain unchallenged, while those who in deep love for Christ, and a burden for His church, and who stand against the apostasy and the sin, face the severest of church discipline.

Manifestly, the parable of the tares confirms that God's church will retain many obviously unfaithful members until the shaking and the sifting have been completed.

8

The Foolish Virgins

One of the most solemn parables in all the Bible is the parable of the foolish virgins. This parable gives deep insights into the end time remnant church. Unlike the tares, who cannot hide their lack of conversion and sincerity indefinitely, the foolish virgins have been a part of God's end time people and always remain sincere. The similarities between the foolish virgins and the wise virgins are amazing.

Both the wise and the foolish are categorized as "virgins." Each wears a white robe (*Christ's Object Lessons,* p. 305). These facts certify that they have not accepted the wine of Babylon; they have not gone a whoring after the fallen churches of Protestantism.

> They are called virgins because they profess a pure faith
> (*Christ's Object Lessons,* p.406).

Too many sincere Seventh-day Adventists believe that the foolish virgins are liberals and apostates within God's church. But God always declares such to be harlots, not virgins.

> They say, if a man put away his wife, and she go from him, and become another man's, shall he return unto her again? shall not that land be greatly polluted? but thou has played the harlot with many lovers; yet return again to me, saith the LORD. Lift up thine eyes unto the high places, and see where thou hast not been lien with. In the ways hast thou sat for them, as the Arabian in the wilderness; and thou hast polluted the land with thy whoredoms and with thy wickedness. Therefore the showers have been withholden, and there hath been no latter rain; and thou hadst a whore's forehead, thou refusedst to be ashamed. Wilt thou not from this time cry unto me, My father, thou art the guide of my youth? Will he reserve his anger for ever? will he keep it to the end? Behold, thou hast spoken and done evil things as thou couldest
>
> (Jeremiah 3:1–5).

The startling fact is that the foolish virgins are to be found among those who believe and proclaim God's precious truths and who are enthusiastic in their fellowship with those of like faith, irrespective of the scorn, ridicule and ecclesiastical persecution they receive. They appreciate present truth and are prepared to travel vast distances to hear it proclaimed. But there has been no transformation of character by the indwelling Spirit.

What a warning this is to those who falsely teach that unless we persistently reject salvation, eternal life is ours, already bestowed at the cross. The foolish virgins *never* rejected salvation. They eagerly desired it. "Lord, Lord, open to us" (Matthew 25:11) was their plaintive and futile plea. They lost eternity not because they rejected it, not because they failed to study books promoting it nor because they did not view video presentations or listen to audio tapes of faithful speakers presenting salvation messages. Neither did they neglect, while possible, to attend truth-filled messages. They shared the truth. But they failed to permit the Holy Spirit to mould their lives in preparation for heaven.

1. The foolish virgins have clearly remained true and faithful to the Word of God.

> So with the church that lives just before Christ's second coming. All have a knowledge of the Scriptures. All have heard the message of Christ's near approach, and confidently expect His appearing   (*Christ's Object Lessons*, p. 408).

2. Both the wise and the foolish initially had a lighted lamp. Scripture declares that the lamp is the Word of God, and the fact that the lamp was lighted is evidence that they had once studied God's Word under the guidance of the Holy Spirit.

> Thy word is a lamp unto my feet, and a light unto my path
>   (Psalm 119:105).

3. All unquestionably were students of God's Word and, at least initially, even the foolish had the Holy Spirit with them, otherwise their lamps would not have been lighted. They all had been under the power of the Holy Spirit, and they all had "vessels for oil" (ibid., p. 408).

4. They were not without a preparation to receive the Holy Spirit. But somehow, during the delay in the return of Jesus they had not refilled their vessels with oil. This neglect had left them unready for the return of Jesus Christ, for they had not received the latter rain.

What a fearful warning this is to God's faithful people! As the delay in the return of Jesus continues, many faithful people will lose the infilling of the power of the Holy Spirit. They will still believe the truth, they will still be considered strong supporters of the truth, but the Holy Spirit is not retained in their heart, and eventually,

> They will fall under the masterful temptations of Satan
> (ibid., p. 411).

5. The foolish virgins are sincere.

> The class represented by the foolish virgins are not hypocrites
> (ibid.).

Therefore these lost ones are not insincere and indifferent. They have a desire to be saved, they are earnest, but without the power of the Holy Spirit they are not prepared for salvation.

6. They know the truth, for they have studied it, and have accepted it.

> They have a regard for the truth (ibid.).

The foolish virgins do not fail of the kingdom because they have neglected the daily study of God's Word. In so many ways they are identical with the wise virgins.

7. The foolish virgins have been witnesses of the truth to others and it is very possible that they may have led others to the kingdom of heaven, for the servant of the Lord says, "they have advocated the truth" (ibid.).

In their more enthusiastic days, the foolish virgins, when they believed that the coming of the Lord was near, were earnest in their witnessing of the truth, but as Christ appeared to linger they became less earnest in their endeavors.

8. These foolish virgins are among those who do believe the truth. For, "They are attracted to those who believe the truth" (ibid.).

We have many times wondered how many of those to whom we preach are really foolish rather than wise virgins. This is a deep burden upon our souls, for our earnest desire is to see no foolish virgins among our listeners.

As we look at the foolish virgins, there is one and one only ingredient lacking for their entrance into the kingdom of heaven. They "took no oil with them" (Matt. 25:3).

> But they have not yielded themselves to the Holy Spirit's working. They have not fallen upon the Rock, Christ Jesus, and permitted their old nature to be broken up. This class are represented also by the stony-ground hearers. They receive the word with readiness, but they fail of assimilating its principles. Its influence is not abiding. The Spirit works upon man's heart, according to his desire and consent implanting in him a new nature; but the class represented by the foolish virgins have been content with a superficial work. They do not know God. They have not studied His character; they have not held communion with Him; therefore they do not know how to trust, how to look and live. Their service to God degenerates into a form   (*Christ's Object Lessons,* p.411).

We fear that many who are foolish virgins do irreparable damage to the cause of truth and righteousness, because they have not come under the power of the Holy Spirit, and yet have a fervor for the truth. They are likely to present the truth in a way that is militant and aggressive, thus failing to exhibit a spirit of Christlikeness. They engender hatred, anger, hostility, and bitterness against those who have not accepted the fullness of God's truth. Rather than taking the opportunity to woo others to Jesus Christ, they turn them away, often never to return. It is only under the power of the Holy Spirit that we have the true transformation of life that is needed for all those who will bring the gospel to the world.

> Seeing ye have purified your souls in obeying the truth through the Spirit unto unfeigned love of the brethren, see that ye love one another with a pure heart fervently: being born again, not of corruptible seed, but of incorruptible, by the word of God, which liveth and abideth for ever (1 Peter 1:22, 23).

This passage of Peter represents a description of the wise virgins. It will be noted that when the foolish virgins came asking them for oil it was too late. We cannot have oil for another. Each one of us has available to him or her the Holy Spirit. If we do not accept the power of the Holy Spirit in our lives there is no way that we can properly represent our Saviour. Therefore our efforts, even when proclaiming an unadulterated truth, present such an unattractive picture of the truth that those who otherwise would be hearers are discouraged and turn away.

It is to be remembered that the Holy Spirit has a two-part work to fulfill in the life of every Christian. Jesus explained the Holy Spirit's first work during His earthly ministry.

> Howbeit when he, the Spirit of truth, is come, he will guide you into all truth: for he shall not speak of himself; but whatsoever he shall hear, that shall he speak: and he will shew you things to come (John 16:13).

It is the Holy Spirit who, if we ask, will protect us from deceptive error. But it would seem that there are many of us who, having received the impartation of the Word of God through the ministry of the Spirit to our mind, fail to allow that same Spirit to transform our lives through the truth, for that is also the work of the Holy Spirit.

> And hope maketh not ashamed; because the love of God is shed abroad in our hearts by the Holy Ghost which is given unto us (Romans 5:5).

Perhaps the foolish virgins are the most tragic of all the lost. They have been so close and so near to the kingdom of heaven, but they have lost eternal life. It is our urgent appeal to our fellow truth-loving believers that, with us, each will examine his or her own life in the light of Calvary and the Scripture and yield to the power of the Holy Spirit to transform the life and make each heart tender and loving while courageous and unwavering.

9

The Sifting and the Shaking

There can be no question that the Seventh-day Adventist Church is now deeply into the shaking time. Both the Bible and the Spirit of Prophecy have given ample evidence that just before the return of Jesus, His people will be shaken and sifted so that only those who are fully committed to the Lord will remain in God's fold.

> But who may abide the day of his coming? and who shall stand when he appeareth? for he is like a refiner's fire, and like fullers' soap: and he shall sit as a refiner and purifier of silver: and he shall purify the sons of Levi, and purge them as gold and silver, that they may offer unto the Lord an offering in righteousness (Malachi 3:2–4).

It is important for those who have considered calling men and women out of the Seventh-day Adventist Church to be extremely careful, for the very last cleansing does not come from a calling out. There is no doubt that the Christian church had to "come out" from the Jewish church, and the Protestant church from out of the Catholic church, and the Seventh-day Adventist Church from out of the Protestant churches. It is then logically concluded by many that now that the Seventh-day Adventist Church is in such deep apostasy, the faithful must therefore leave the Seventh-day Adventist Church. And while this may appear to be logical, a little reflection will reveal the danger of such a conclusion.

If God's faithful people were to separate from the Seventh-day Adventist Church, soon that new church would be in apostasy, and another coming out would be required, and so on, *ad infinitum*. The Lord would never return to take home His saints. God in His wisdom had chosen a better way for the cleansing of the final generation of His people, and that is the shaking and the sifting.

If we genuinely believe that we must come out of the Seventh-day Adventist Church now, we are certainly throwing the day of Christ's return off into the future and are effectively joining those who declare, "my Lord delayeth His coming." Every sign that we can see bespeaks the fact that Jesus is coming back very soon. We are in the time of the end of this world's history. Surely every perceptive Seventh-day Adventist should understand the times in which we live.

> But ye, brethren, are not in darkness, that that day should overtake you as a thief. Ye are all the children of light, and the children of the day: we are not of the night, nor of darkness. Therefore let us not sleep, as do others; but let us watch and be sober. For they that sleep sleep in the night; and they that be drunken are drunken in the night. But let us, who are of the day, be sober, putting on the breastplate of faith and love; and for an helmet, the hope of salvation. For God hath not appointed us to wrath, but to obtain salvation by our Lord Jesus Christ (1 Thessalonians 5:4–9).

This shaking, sifting time is meant to test the fullness of the loyalty and veracity of every professing Seventh-day Adventist. Tragically, many will defect from the side of Christ and join the spiritualistic banner of Satan.

> Now the Spirit speaketh expressly, that in the latter times some shall depart from the faith, giving heed to seducing spirits, and doctrines of devils (1 Timothy 4:1).

It will be noted that this text is dealing with the latter times. There are going to be those who depart from "the faith." Thus this group once believed the truth that God has entrusted to this church. But in the end, they believe the doctrines of devils and give heed to seducing spirits. What a terrible tragedy this is!

What a solemn warning this is to those who are fascinated by the use of the Ericsonian hypnotic techniques of neurolinguistic programs (NLP) in the Lab I and II courses promoted by many of our Conferences, and the Spiritualistic concepts of the false Holy Spirit promoted by the Celebration (Charismatic) Movement even in General Conference publications (for example the October 1991 issue of the *Ministry* magazine.

Now, we understand the way in which we will be shaken. Inspiration details three stages of the shaking. The first is the introduction of false theories into the church.

> When the shaking comes, by the introduction of false theories, the surface readers, anchored nowhere, are like shifting sand *(Testimonies to Ministers,* p. 112).

> God will arouse His people; if other means fail, heresies will come in among them, which will sift them, separating the chaff from the wheat *(Testimonies,* vol. 5, p. 707).

This stage is almost fully matured in the church today.

We wonder how many more heresies could possibly come into God's church. But we know that every possible heresy will come because the testimony of God says,

> The days are fast approaching when there will be great perplexity and confusion. Satan, clothed in angel's robes will deceive, if possible, the very elect. There will be gods many and lords many. Every wind of doctrine will be blowing
> *(Testimonies,* vol. 5, p. 80).

We can be assured from this that every possible belief of the Seventh-day Adventist Church will be severely tested. We have seen the attack on the sanctuary message and the investigative judgment. We have seen the attack on Christ Our Righteousness and on the humanity of Jesus Christ. We have seen the diminution of regard for the Sabbath, but we can rest assured that there will be those that will arise strongly denouncing the Sabbath and the other great pillars of our faith, including the state of the dead and the Second Coming of Jesus. Nothing will be left untouched during this shaking period, as Satan seeks to deceive the very elect. It is patently clear that only those who are under the daily guidance of the Holy Spirit and are earnestly studying God's Word will be able to resist the persuasiveness of these deceptions.

While there have always been assaults upon God's church, there is no doubt that the greatest assault began when the dialogues with Evangelical Protestants convened in the 1950s. The fruit of that dialogue has continued to advance with frightening rapidity until it would seem that most Seventh-day Adventists no longer know, let alone believe, the glorious everlasting gospel that God has entrusted to them. Thus they are wholly defenseless against the artful temptations and deceptions of Satan.

The second stage of the shaking deals with the presentation of the straight testimony to the church of Laodicea.

> I asked the meaning of the shaking I had seen, and was shown that it would be caused by the straight testimony called forth by the counsel of true witness to the Laodiceans. This will have its effect upon the heart of the receiver, and will lead him to exalt the standard and pour forth the straight truth. Some will not bear this testimony. They will rise up against it, and this will cause a shaking among God's people
> *(Testimonies,* vol. 1, p. 181).

The Laodicean message is a message that God has given to bring His church back to its position of upright distinction from the world. The description of this church is dramatic and tragic.

> Because thou sayest, I am rich, and increased with goods, and have need of nothing: and knowest not that thou art wretched, and miserable, and poor, and blind, and naked
> (Revelation 3:17).

What a frightening description of the church that God has chosen to bear the banner of truth throughout the whole world at the end of time! But this message is not a message of rejection, as some suggest. It is a message of love, and God has given the antidote to this terrible malaise in His church.

> I counsel thee to buy of me gold [divine faith and love] tried in the fire, that thou mayest be rich, and white raiment [the garment of Christ's perfect righteousness], that thou mayest be clothed, and that the shame of thy nakedness do not appear; and anoint thine eyes with eyesalve [the enlightenment of truth, spiritual discernment under the power of the indwelling Holy Spirit], that thou mayest see   (Rev. 3:18).

As faithful messengers give this message, many will rise up to oppose it and, rather than accepting the message, they will accuse the messengers of preaching a discouraging message and focusing too much upon the negatives. But God's faithful messengers must give the warning. Some will accept their message, and this message will lead God's people into the kingdom of heaven. There have been those who have said that we will have to come back to the church of Philadelphia, a position that a few of the pioneers held for awhile, but the servant of the Lord makes it plain that this is not true, for she says,

> Those who come up to every point, and stand every test, and overcome, be the price what it may, have heeded the counsel of true witness, and they will receive the latter rain, and thus be fitted for translation (*Testimonies,* vol. 1, p. 187).

This beautiful message to Laodicea, the final appeal of God to His people, is a glorious message. God does not spew Laodicea out of His mouth as many say, because He stands at the door and knocks. He has promised,

> If any man hear my voice, and open the door, I will come in to him, and will sup with him, and he with me
> (Revelation 3:20).

There is a glorious promise to the overcomer.

> To him that overcometh will I grant to sit with me in my throne, even as I also overcame, and am set down with my Father in His throne (Revelation 3:21).

The third and final stage of the shaking and sifting is persecution. This is not referring to the persecution of the time of Jacob's trouble, which comes subsequent to the close of human probation, but to the persecution referred to as the little time of trouble. Some people have misunderstood this to be a time of little trouble, but indeed it is a short time of terrible persecution, as Satan in his final efforts seeks to destroy all God's faithful saints.

> When the law of God is made void the church will be sifted by fiery trials, and a larger proportion than we now anticipate, will give heed to seducing spirits and doctrines of devils. Instead of being strengthened when brought into strait places, many prove that they are not living branches of the True Vine; they bore no fruit, and the husbandman taketh them away (*Selected Messages,* Book. 2, p. 368).

It is during this final test that the last of those who have not wholly surrendered their wills to Christ, who have not overcome "by the blood of the Lamb and the word of their testimony" (Revelation 12:11) are swept aside, leaving only those who have unreservedly committed their lives and wills to God. Persecution will be fearful.

> Nations will be stirred to their very center. Support will be withdrawn from those who proclaim God's only standard of righteousness, the only sure test of character. And all who will not bow to the decree of the national councils and obey the national laws to exalt the sabbath instituted by the man of sin, to the disregard of God's holy day, will feel, not the oppressive power of popery alone, but of the Protestant world, the image of the beast   (*Selected Messages,* Book 2, p. 380).

There will be many of our readers, especially those who are older, who have seen the ancient ways of shaking and sifting the harvested grain by hand. The grain is placed in a container, the bottom of which consists of a grate. The purpose of the sieve is to shake out the husks and the chaff, leaving only the pure grain fully separated from that which is worthless. The farmer throws the wheat into the air in a shaking fashion, and then by a rotating action, moves the grain each way as the chaff and the husks fall to the ground. It is not uncommon, even for the most expert individual, for a few of the grains to fall to the ground. But God has promised that in His sifting, shaking of God's remnant people, such will never occur.

> For, lo, I will command, and I will sift the house of Israel among all nations, like as corn is sifted in a sieve, yet shall not the least grain fall upon the earth   (Amos 9:9).

God will not make any mistakes in the shaking and sifting time. The pure grain, those who have allowed Christ total access to their lives, will not be lost. But those who have sought by human invention, or have been indifferent, will be shaken out of God's remnant church.

God cannot redeem His saints until the shaking has taken place.

> And this word, Yet once more, signifieth the removing of those things that are shaken, as of things that are made, that those things which cannot be shaken may remain
> (Hebrews 12:27).

Everything is to be shaken that can be shaken
(*Testimonies,* vol. 1, p. 355).

The Sifting and the Shaking

> Soon everything that can be shaken will be shaken, that those things that cannot be shaken may remain
> *(Testimonies,* vol. 9, p. 15–16).

This shaking will be complete and thorough. God's faithful people will face the agonizing experience of seeing the majority of God's people desert from the faith.

> The shaking of God blows away multitudes like dry leaves
> *(Testimonies,* vol. 4, p. 89).

Other people who will be shaken out of God's church are not left in any doubt.

> Then again was held up before me those who were not willing to dispose of this world's goods to save perishing souls by sending them the truth while Jesus stands before the Father pleading His blood, His sufferings, and His death for them; and while God's messengers are waiting, ready to carry them the saving truth that they might be sealed with the seal of the living God. It is hard for some who profess to believe the present truth, to do even so little as to hand the messengers God's own money that He has lent them to be stewards over. . . . The angel said, "Can such enter heavens?" Another angel answered, "No, never, never, never." Those who are not interested in the cause of God on earth, can never sing the song of redeeming love above   *(Early Writings,* p. 49–50).

> Some, I saw, did not participate in this work of agonizing and pleading. They seemed indifferent and careless. They were not resisting the darkness around them, and it shut them in like a thick cloud. The angels of God left these, and I saw them hastening to the assistance of those who were struggling with all their energies to resist the evil angels, and trying to help themselves by calling upon God with perseverance
> *(Testimonies,* vol. 1, p. 180–181).

> The careless and the indifferent, who did not join those who prized victory and salvation enough to perseveringly plead and agonize for it, did not obtain it, and they were left behind in darkness   *(Testimonies,* vol. 1, p. 182).

Surely this is a time for all of us to permit Christ to prepare our hearts wholly for this great testing time ahead. It is further a time when each of us must share the solemn truths of the preparation for the trials ahead and encourage all our fellow believers that it is not a superficial preparation that is needed in this time of crisis. The Lord gives us encouragement and tells us who will be able to stand this fearful sifting and shaking.

> Everything that can be shaken will be shaken; but rooted and grounded in the truth, you will abide with those things that cannot be shaken. The law of God is steadfast, unalterable; for it is the expression of the character of Jehovah. Make up your mind that you will not by word or influence cast the least dishonor upon its authority
> *(Messages to Young People,* p. 30).

At the foundation of loyalty to God is the truth, because

> There is no sanctification aside from the truth
> *(Fundamentals of Christian Education,* p. 432).

> Unity is the sure result of Christian perfection
> *(Sanctified Life,* p. 85).

The unity that God is calling us to obtain is the unity that is built upon the foundation of truth unmodified and unchanged. This is the only surety we have as we face the crises of the end time.

For further encouragement, as myriads defect from God's church during the shaking, others courageously step in to fill their places.

> The careless and indifferent, who did not join with those who prized victory and salvation enough to perseveringly plead and agonize for it, did not obtain it, and they were left behind in darkness, but their numbers were immediately made up by others taking hold of the truth and coming into the ranks
> *(Testimonies,* vol. 1, p. 182).

The fierceness of the battle and the struggle is vividly described.

> In vision I saw two armies in terrible conflict. One army was led by banners bearing the world's insignia; the other was led by the blood-stained banner of Prince Immanuel. Standard after standard was left to trail in the dust as company after company from the Lord's army joined the foe and tribe after tribe from the ranks of the enemy united with the commandment-keeping people of God   *(Testimonies,* vol. 8, p. 41).

What a tragedy that there is such a defection from the ranks of God! But how glorious it is that many come into God's church from the side of Satan during the fierceness of the battle, and join the ranks of Prince Immanuel.

This again is an indication to us that we need to be vigorously proclaiming the everlasting gospel at this time. If we are waiting for a time of peace and unity in the church before we present God's gospel, that will never be; for Satan is going to assault right up to the end of time. But praise God, at the worst time in the history of the Seventh-day Adventist Church, as untold numbers leave the ranks of Christ and join the foes of truth and righteousness, others, who once walked in the darkness and who had been on the side of Satan, join the faithful of God's church. This is not a time to leave God's church, for it is the enemies of truth and righteousness that lead away. How plainly this is described by the prophet Isaiah. It will be noted that it is not those who leave Zion and Jerusalem who will be saved, but those who stay there.

> In that day shall the branch of the LORD be beautiful and glorious, and the fruit of the earth shall be excellent and comely for them that are escaped of Israel. And it shall come to pass, that he that is left in Zion, and he that remaineth in Jerusalem, shall be called holy, even every one that is written among the living in Jerusalem: When the Lord shall have washed away the filth of the daughters of Zion, and shall have purged the blood of Jerusalem from the midst thereof by the spirit of judgment, and by the spirit of burning. And the LORD will create upon every dwelling place of mount Zion, and upon her assemblies, a cloud and smoke by day, and the shining of a flaming fire by night: for upon all the glory shall be a defence. (Isaiah 4:2–5).

It matters not the perspective from which we take it. The Word of God is emphatic that the Seventh-day Adventist Church, fearfully shaken and sifted, buffeted, persecuted, assaulted, is still the vehicle through which God's faithful people will enter the kingdom of heaven. But by the work of God all the unholy will be removed from the church before that takes place and God will have vested leaders who are servants and ministers, not rulers and dictators.

10

The Church Militant, The Church Triumphant

There is no need for us to be confused by the statements of holy inspiration which sometimes refer to God's church as perfect and sometimes as greatly defective. Two statements have been frequently misused by those who would suggest that anyone who is not faithful to God is not a member of God's church.

> God has a church. It is not the great cathedral, neither is it the national establishment, neither is it the various denominations; it is the people who love God and keep His commandments. . . . Where Christ is even among the humble few, this is Christ's church, for the presence of the High and Holy One who inhabiteth eternity can alone constitute a church
> (*Upward Look,* p. 315).

Before this statement was commonly known, there was an other statement from *Acts of the Apostles* which was used by those who separated from the Seventh-day Adventist Church.

> The church is God's fortress, His city of refuge, which He holds in a revolted world. Any betrayal of the church is treachery to Him who has bought mankind with the blood of His only begotten Son. From the beginning, faithful souls have constituted the church on earth. In every age the Lord has had His watchmen, who have born a faithful testimony to the generation in which they lived. These sentinels gave the message of warning; and when they were called to lay off their armor, others took up the work. God brought these witnesses into covenant relation with Himself, uniting the church on earth with the church in heaven. He has sent forth His angels to minister to His church, and the gates of hell have not been able to prevail against His people
> (*Acts of the Apostles,* p. 11).

A little reflection leads us to agree that only true and faithful people will be saved in the kingdom of heaven. It stands to reason that those who have not surrendered their lives wholly to the Lord, though they may have been members of the Israelite nation or the

Jews, were not truly His faithful people. Yet they were counted among the people of God. They were numbered with His people. They were not dismissed from the congregation of Israel, because man would have made many mistakes. There is a chasm of difference between being a member of God's church on earth and being a candidate for the heavenly home.

In the two statements above, the servant of the Lord is plainly dealing with those who will be saved in the kingdom of heaven. If we had only these statements, then we would be justified in drawing the conclusion that anyone who is not fully committed to the Lord is not part of the church, but that conclusion cannot be sustained from Scripture nor the Spirit of Prophecy. We have already pointed out the terrible abominations that were done in Corinth and the apostasy in Galatia, yet both churches were referred to as the church of God. The servant of the Lord, dealing with the apostolic church, comments:

> Early in the history of the church the mystery of iniquity foretold by the apostle Paul began its baleful work; and as the false teachers concerning whom Peter had warned the believers, urged their heresies, many were ensnared by false doctrines. Some faltered under trial, and were tempted to give up the faith. At the time when John was given this revelation, many had lost their first love of gospel truth. But in His mercy God did not leave the church to continue in a backslidden state. In a message of infinite tenderness He revealed His love for them, and His desire that they should make sure work for eternity (Ibid., p. 587).

Sister White further states that

> The church was defective and in need of stern reproof and chastisement; and John was inspired to record messages of warning and reproof and entreaty to those who, losing sight of the fundamental principles of the gospel, should imperil their hope of salvation. But always the words of rebuke that God finds it necessary to send are spoken in tender love, and with the promise of peace to every penitent believer (ibid).

John the beloved indicated that already the work of antichrist was invading the church.

> Little children, it is the last time: and as ye have heard that antichrist shall come, even now are there many antichrists; whereby we know that it is the last time (1 John 2:18).

Of course we know the antichrist was not fully manifested until the development of the Roman Catholic Papacy, nevertheless elements were already in the apostolic church.

Sister White defines two aspects of the church which she refers to as the "church militant" and the "church triumphant." Some of the many statements which Sister White has made concerning the church triumphant and the church militant reveal that the church militant is the present church.

> Has God no living church? He has a church, but it is the church militant, not the church triumphant
> (*Testimonies to Ministers,* p. 45).

On the other hand, the church triumphant is the church redeemed. The church triumphant is always referred to as the church in heaven.

> The church militant is not the church triumphant, and earth is not Heaven (*Signs of the Times,* January 4, 1883).

> The members of the church triumphant,—the church in heaven—will be permitted to draw near to the members of the church militant, to aid them in their necessity
> (*The Southern Watchman,* September 8, 1903).

> The church militant is not in this world the church triumphant (*Review and Herald,* July 26, 1898).

We are given much counsel concerning the church militant.

1. Carnally minded people will be in the church militant.

> Let every one who is seeking to live a Christian life, remember that the church militant is not the church triumphant. Those who are carnally minded will be found in the church. They are to be pitied more than blamed. The church is not to be judged as sustaining these characters, though they are found within her borders. Should the church expel them, the very ones who found fault with their presence there, would blame the church for sending them adrift in the world; they would claim that they were treated unmercifully. It may be that in the church there are those who are cold, proud, haughty, and

The Church Militant, The Church Triumphant 69

un-Christian, but you need not associate with this class. There are many who are warm-hearted, who are self-denying, self-sacrificing, who would, were it required, lay down their lives to save souls. Jesus saw the bad and the good in church relationship, and said, "Let both grow together until the harvest" *(Review and Herald,* January 16, 1894).

2. Satan's agents are more active than God's agents in the church militant.

We wish we had heaven here below, but we have not. The church militant is not the church triumphant. The church militant must wrestle and toil. She must strive against temptations and fight severe battles, because Satan is not dead. His agencies are much more active in his work than are the agencies of God in the work of their Leader
(General Conference Bulletin, April 22, 1901).

3. The church militant contains defective members.

Has God no living church? He has a church but it is the church militant, not the church triumphant. We are sorry that there are defective members, that there are tares amid the wheat *(Testimonies to Ministers,* p. 45).

Now we ask the question, What will we do in relationship to these unfaithful members? There is very important counsel for us in this regard.

It may be that in the church there are those who are cold, proud, haughty, and un-Christian, but you need not associate with this class. There are many who are warmhearted, who are self-denying, self-sacrificing, who would, were it required, lay down their lives to save souls. . . . None are under the necessity of becoming tares because every plant in the field is not wheat. If the truth were known, these complainers make their accusations in order to quiet a convicted, condemning conscience. Their own course of action is not wholly commendable. Even those who are striving for the mastery over the enemy, have sometimes been wrong and done wrong. Evil prevails over good when we do not trust wholly in Christ, and abide in Him *(Review and Herald,* January 16, 1894).

This battle between good and evil reaches its greatest magnitude, not in the world, but in the church. For it is the church that is the major object of Satan's assaults.

> While Christ is sowing the good seed, Satan is sowing the tares. There are two opposing influences continually exerted on the members of the church. One influence is working for the purification of the church, and the other for the corrupting of the people of God (*The Faith I Live By*, p. 305).

It is essential for us to prepare new members in a way that they will understand the implications of the terrible schisms within God's church. Nothing can be more harmful than to hasten people into Seventh-day Adventist Church membership thinking that its members live the ideals of God. Such new members, because of ignorance and lack of thorough preparation, are likely to become enemies of truth and agents of Satan.

There is another concern that needs to be addressed. Many in preparing people for the membership in God's remnant church have done nothing to prepare these people for the terrible apostasy that they will witness once they join the church. Thus, many come into the church with rose-tinted glasses, believing that everyone will be on fire for the Lord and all will be proceding heavenward. It is essential that these people be thoroughly prepared for the state in which they will encounter the church. We have found that when we have done this, we do not often lose souls. We explain that Satan's wrath is against the Seventh-day Adventist Church. We explain that many of Satan's agents are in the Seventh-day Adventist Church. We detail to them many of the problems that they are going to find. But we also explain that the Seventh-day Adventist Church *is* the remnant church; that this is the church that God is cleansing so that He might have a perfect church before Christ returns. We explain emphatically that God's truth is deposited in this church and can be found in no other church.

Colin well remembers his dialogue with a fellow minister many years ago. This pastor was seeking to bring into the Seventh-day Adventist Church a woman who belonged to one of the established churches of Canada. Her own minister was alarmed and asked the opportunity to dialogue with the minister with whom she was studying. That meeting was arranged, and during the course of that dialogue, the lady's minister asked, "Are you saying that the Seventh-day Adventist Church contains all the truth?" The Seventh-day Adventist minister replied, "No, I can never say that." Then turning to the woman, her pastor said, "Well, we do not believe that we have all the truth, this man does not believe his church has all the truth, there is no point in moving into his church." The Seventh-day Adventist minister turned to the lady's minister and said, "But I have not completed what I intended to say. It is true that the Seventh-day Adventist church does not have all the truth, for only God has all the truth. But all that we have is truth."

In commenting upon the response of people who had not been prepared for what they will find in the church, we have this counsel,

> Some people seem to think that upon entering the church they will have their expectations fulfilled, and meet only with those who are pure and perfect. They are zealous in their faith, and when they see faults in church members, they say, "We left the world in order to have no association with evil characters, but the evil is here also"; and they ask, as did the servants in the parable, "From whence then hath it tares?" But we need not be thus disappointed, for the Lord has not warranted us in coming to the conclusion that the church is perfect; and all our zeal will not be successful in making the church militant as pure as the church triumphant. The Lord forbids us to proceed in any violent way against those whom we think erring, and we are not to deal out excommunications and denunciations to those who are faulty
>
> (*Testimonies to Ministers*, p. 47).

The Lord has given us further warnings concerning those who make their main object an assault upon the Seventh-day Adventist Church.

> When men arise, claiming to have a message from God, but instead of warring against principalities and powers, and the rulers of the darkness of this world, they form a hollow square, and turn the weapons of warfare against the church militant, be afraid of them. They do not bear the divine credentials. God has not given them any such burden of labor. They would tear down that which God would restore by the Laodicean

message. He wounds only that he may heal, not cause to perish. The Lord lays upon no man a message that will discourage and dishearten the church. He reproves, he rebukes, he chastens; but it is only that he might restore and approve at last (*Review and Herald,* October 17, 1893).

It seems to us, then, that we need to be careful even as we point out the serious scandals and flaws in God's remnant church. We need to have the same goals that God has. If there be wounding it is to heal and if there be reproof, rebuke, and entreaties, it is to restore. There can be no joy in reporting some of the situations in our church. We believe it wise to avoid widespread presentations of personal scandals of members and ministers, and even leaders in the church. While recognizing that we have a God-given responsibility to be watchmen on the walls of Zion, to warn men and women concerning doctrinal error, and to call men and women to the fullness of godly repentance, there is little to be said for making the numerous scandals in our church the focus of our ministry.

The above message of the Lord's messenger was read at the 1893 General Conference session. It was at this session that a number of people were scattering leaflets denouncing the Seventh-day Adventist Church as Babylon. The messenger of God said,

> How is it that these pamphlets denouncing the Seventh-day Adventist Church as Babylon were scattered abroad everywhere, at the very time when that church was receiving the outpouring of the Spirit of God? How is it that men can be so deceived as to imagine that the loud cry consists in calling the people of God out from the fellowship of a church that is enjoying a season of refreshing? Oh, may these deceived souls come into the current, and receive the blessing, and be endued with power from on high (ibid).

While it may not yet be that the Holy Spirit is being poured out upon the church once again, still we believe that we have come to the time of the latter rain, and that God is clearly identifying a people who are ready to receive the outpouring of the Holy Spirit. Around the world we see men and women being enlightened and reshaping their lives under the power of the Holy Spirit, ready for the latter rain. This is not a time to declare the Seventh-day Adventist Church to be Babylon, rather it is a time for personal

The Church Militant, The Church Triumphant 73

preparation. We have emphasized that the message concerning Babylon is not for the Seventh-day Adventist Church, but rather it is the Laodicean message that we all need today. That message is a call for all God's faithful people to be ready to receive the approbation of God, the sealing of their lives and the ministration of the Holy Spirit in a power greater than Pentecost. This should be the major focus of all God's faithful people today.

As we are still in the time of the church militant, God's faithful servants have a critical work to do for the church.

> The church is composed of erring men and women who will need patient, painstaking effort, that they may be educated, trained, and disciplined by precept and example, to do their work with acceptance here in this life, and to be crowned with glory and immortality in the future life
>
> (*EGW 1888 materials,* p. 249).

> We are as a church to be wide awake, and to work for the erring among us, as laborers together with God. We are furnished with spiritual weapons, mighty to the pulling down of the fortress of the enemy. We are not to hurl the thunderbolts against the church of Christ militant; for Satan is doing all he possibly can on this line, and you who claim to be the remnant of the people of God had better not be found helping him, denouncing, accusing and condemning. Seek to restore, not to tear down, discourage and destroy
>
> (*Manuscript Release,* vol. 1, p. 357).

This is a restorative work. Those who constantly chide church members for their lack of spiritual understanding and worldly lifestyle, are rarely able to do the major work that God has called us to do. We must reprove and rebuke "with all longsuffering and doctrine" (2 Timothy 4:2). This is a work that all of us must enter into. This is not a work of denouncing the church as Babylon, although we do know that as apostate Israel, we are vastly more culpable than Babylon can ever be.

> There is but one church in the world who are at the present time standing in the breach, and making up the hedge, building up the old waste places; and for any man to call the attention of the world and other churches to this church, denouncing her as Babylon, is to do a work in harmony with him who is the accuser of the brethren. Is it possible that men

> will arise from among us, who speak perverse things, and give voice to the very sentiments that Satan would have disseminated in the world in regard to those who keep the commandments of God, and have the faith of Jesus? Is there not work enough to satisfy your zeal in presenting the truth to those who are in the darkness of error? As those who have been made stewards of means and ability, you have been misapplying your Lord's goods in disseminating error
> (*Review and Herald,* September 5, 1893).

We have a burden for those who take the problems of the church to the world. If we have a love for the Seventh-day Adventist Church, we will not be guilty of exposing the failures of the church to the world. The Seventh-day Adventist Church, to us, is our family, and though we have deep concerns, this is not something to share with the world at large. We need to be protective of this church which God has raised up in these last times to take the message of hope to the world. Any effort to scandalize the Seventh-day Adventist Church before the world is a terrible dishonor to God and will result in many never again looking to this church for the answer to their spiritual needs.

We can rest assured that we will have divine aid as we reach out to others, seeking to bring them to the precious truths that God has entrusted to us.

> The members of the church triumphant,—the church in heaven—will be permitted to draw near to the members of the church militant, to aid them in their necessity. Let us ever remember we are laborers together with God. In this heavenly union we shall carry forward His work with completeness, with singing and rejoicing. In every soul will be kindled the fire of holy zeal. Company after company will leave the dark standard of the foe, to come up to the help of the Lord
> (*The Southern Watchman,* September 8, 1903).

Oh, how beautifully God has given us our commission! There are too many today focusing so intently upon the scandals of the church that they are doing nothing to bring men and women into the church. Some argue that this is no time to bring people into the church and therefore no time to do missionary outreach and evangelism. But we say this is the greatest time to do such work. It is up to God whether to bring our contacts into the church or not, but we must share the gospel. We must not excuse our indolence on the basis of the state of the church. If it is not the time to bring them in, God will hold them back till the right time, and no doubt, when the faithful of Babylon are called into the fold of God, these people will take their stand openly and forthrightly for truth.

Few accepted the invitation of Jesus while He was on earth, but under the power of the early rain, many of those who had been greatly moved by Jesus, openly accepted the gospel and joined the persecuted ones in proclaiming Christ as their Lord and Saviour. This is a time for us to do everything we can to influence men and women for the truth so that when that time comes, and the Lord has cleansed His church and it is safe to bring them in, He will be able to do so.

As we come to the end of earth's probation, there will be great persecution against the church militant.

> The time in which we live is a time when the church militant will realize the oppressive power of persecution, because they keep the Sabbath of Creation, which God has sanctified and blessed *(Manuscript Release, vol. 5, p. 84).*

Let it not be those of us who are part of the church militant to create such an environment and to stir up such antagonism and animosity that we are responsible for the persecution that comes upon us. It is one thing to be persecuted for righteousness' sake; it is an entirely different thing to be persecuted because of hostility and impetuousness.

We recognize that whatever we do, even the most godly acts and words will be misrepresented, but we must not be responsible for bringing the time of trouble upon us.

> They can misrepresent the words and actions of the faithful servants of God, who strive to place the straying feet of the erring in the path of holiness. They can put the worst construction on the words and actions of those who labor for the erring. If they are not converted, if they do not choose to put away their evil speaking, if they corrupt their ways before the Lord, they will misinterpret the word of God's servants, and the whole world will rise up in the day of judgment against them *(Manuscript Release, vol. 7, p. 177).*

Being a part of the church militant is not an easy role. Only a small remnant of the church militant will one day become the church triumphant, the church united with the beings of the universe who have never succumbed to sin nor to transgression. The faithful will become the church triumphant, the perfect church, the church that never again will yield to any disloyalty or disobedience to God.

> The work is soon to close. The members of the church militant who have proved faithful will become the church triumphant (*Evangelism*, p. 707).

Above all, it should be our focus and our burden to become part of the church triumphant and to help others on their pilgrimage towards the heavenly home.

We have presented God's inspired words concerning the church militant. In doing this we in no wise seek to uplift corrupt administrative practices and policies within God's church. We do not purpose to direct people within the Lord's church to accept the words of men who propose matters contrary to the plain Word of God. To do so would be to ignore the penetrating lessons of the history of the first advent. It is an act of total disloyalty to our God to place loyalty to church leaders and organization before loyalty to our God and His truth. Yet such is frequently sponsored in God's church and even more frequently followed by the majority of laity. Error is not sanctified by its support from church leaders or church committees. Error is ever error. We do not demand that God's people sit in the pews of the church week after week to have their souls assaulted by error. Such would dishonor our God.

> My message to you is: No longer consent to listen without protest to the perversion of truth. Unmask the pretentious sophistries which, if received, will lead ministers and physicians and medical missionary workers to ignore the truth. Every one is now to stand on his guard. God calls upon men and women to take their stand under the blood-stained banner of Prince Emmanuel. I have been instructed to warn our people; for many are in danger of receiving theories and sophistries that undermine the foundation pillars of the faith
> (*Selected Messages*, book I, p. 196, 197).

11
Ancient Babylon and Ancient Israel

Faced with so much evidence of apostasy, worldliness, and complacency in the Seventh-day Adventist Church, many have been led to believe, or at least entertain the thought, that the Seventh-day Adventist Church is now Babylon. Much can be learned from an understanding of the way the Lord dealt with both ancient Babylon and ancient Israel. From this study we may understand how God is dealing with apostate Christianity and Seventh-day Adventism today. A view of the history of Babylon and of Israel provides a secure foundation for our understanding of God's dealings with both nations. The Israelites rose out of the bosom of Abraham. Abraham was a man who dutifully responded in faith to the call of God, to separate himself from the rampaging apostasy and paganism of his day.

> Now the LORD had said unto Abram, Get thee out of thy country, and from thy kindred, and from thy father's house, unto a land that I will shew thee: and I will make of thee a great nation, and I will bless thee, and make thy name great; and thou shalt be a blessing: and I will bless them that bless thee, and curse him that curseth thee; and in thee shall all families of the earth be blessed (Genesis 12:1–2).

The response of Abraham was immediate,

> So Abram departed, as the LORD had spoken unto him
> (Genesis 12:4).

In ultimate loyalty to the Word of God, Abraham had been willing to sacrifice his only son, Isaac. Genesis 22:9–12. Through the lineage of Isaac began the Israelite nation. This nation, chosen of God, was called not only to be faithful to Him, to His Word, and to His righteousness, but to carry the flame of truth to all peoples of the world.

The history of Babylon is altogether different. It began with the rebellion of Nimrod. Nimrod was a warrior and a conqueror, and began to establish cities in his own honor.

> And Cush begat Nimrod: he began to be a mighty one in the earth. He was a mighty hunter before the LORD; wherefore it is said, Even as Nimrod the mighty hunter before the LORD. And the beginning of his kingdom was Babel [Babylon], and Erech, and Accad, and Calneh in the land Shinar. Out of that land went forth Asshur [margin, he went out into Assyria], and builded Nineveh, and the city Rehoboth, and Calah, and Resen between Nineveh and Calah: the same is a great city
> (Genesis 10:8–12).

Nimrod (or as he is referred to in history, Ninus, or Nimrud), was responsible for the establishment of two great civilizations, the Babylonian and the Assyrian. For 1500 years they dominated the world, a period longer than the dominion of any other civilization in the history of the planet. Both were built upon paganism, and were in direct rebellion against God. It was at Babylon that these pagan rebels began to build a great ziggurat that they hoped would reach to heaven. This symbolized their faithlessness in rejecting God's promise that never again would the whole world be deluged by a flood. However the rebellion was much deeper than this, for it was an attempt by man to reach heaven by human works. This became the basis of all pagan religions. Babylon became the archetype of religions, not only in the Persian gulf, but in Phoenicia, Egypt, Canaan, Greece, Rome, and ultimately reaching to India, China and the Americas and the utmost bounds of the earth.

To Israel God entrusted the depository of His truth, the oracles of faith and righteousness. Babylon presents the pagan, satanic challenge to that truth of God. Down through the history of the world, Babylon never accepted the truth that would bring men and women to salvation. Its whole philosophy was built upon the deception of Satan—a mingling of truth with error, good with evil. It was established upon balancing the cosmic forces in the universe, including good and evil, and truth and error. The oracles of God, however, had been placed with Israel, first in verbal form, and later in written form. It was God's plan that His people, Israel, and later, the Jews, would be the missionaries who would take this gospel of salvation to the world, turning the pagans to believers and worshipers of the true God. It was God's purpose that,

Ancient Babylon and Ancient Israel

In thee shall all families of the earth be blessed   (Genesis 12:3).

But, the history of Israel and Judah is a sad history. Rather than fulfilling the great mission that God had intrusted to them as His chosen people, they themselves became enmeshed with the influence of paganism and never accomplished the purpose for which God had called them. Yet it is important to acknowledge that never were Israel and Judah ever called Babylon, though they had fallen back into the deepest apostasy. If one were considering Israel just prior to the Assyrian captivity, it would have been extraordinarily difficult to find the difference between Israel and pagan Assyria. It will be recalled that after the division of the kingdom, when only the two tribes of Judah and Benjamin remained faithful to the rightful heir, Rehoboam the son of Solomon, that Jeroboam, the usurper, led the northern kingdom of Israel back into calf worship and idolatry. There was never again to be a king of Israel who would lead the people back to God. All kings were idolaters, and corrupt in their rulership. On the other hand, the smaller kingdom of Judah had an up-and-down experience. Many of Judah's kings were, for the most part, faithful to God, including the first four kings, Rehoboam, Abijah, Asa, and Jehosephat, and some of the later kings including Hezekiah, Joash, and Josiah. Yet it is a stunning revelation that God actually preferred Israel to Judah. He preferred the nation that never once turned to Him, to the nation that had an up-and-down experience.

> And yet for all this her treacherous sister Judah hath not turned unto me with her whole heart, but feignedly, saith the LORD. And the Lord said unto me, The backsliding Israel hath justified herself more than treacherous Judah
> (Jeremiah 3:10, 11).

This, when properly understood, is the Laodicean message in the Old Testament. God says of Laodicea:

> I know thy works, that thou art neither cold nor hot: I would thou wert cold or hot   (Revelation 3:15).

God actually preferred the wholly non-responsive Israel to Judah, with its half-hearted and spasmodic response. Both Israel and Judah completely failed in the mission that God had called them to fulfill. This led to the disappearance of the kingdom of Israel, after the Assyrian captivity, but God still persevered with Judah until after the crucifixion of our Lord and Saviour. Even in their deepest apostasy, God sent His prophets to these abominable apostate nations. In reality, Israel and Judah were far more culpable in their apostasy than Babylon or Assyria. They had had great light: God had entrusted the clearest truth to them and they still rejected it. Always apostate Israel (ancient or modern) is far more to be condemned than is Babylon. Israel is always the depositary of God's truth, and there is no excuse for rejection nor neglect of the salvation that God offered. On the other hand, Babylon, and those in Babylon, do not have such privileges, and therefore their rebellion is far more understandable. This truth led to the most scathing condemnations upon Israel and Judah by the prophets of old. Isaiah used the strongest of language.

> How is the faithful city become an harlot! it was full of judgment; righteousness lodged in it; but now murderers. Thy silver is become dross, thy wine mixed with water: thy princes are rebellious, and companions of thieves: every one loveth gifts, and followeth after rewards: they judge not the fatherless, neither doth the cause of the widow come unto them
> (Isaiah 1:21–23).

The persecuted Jeremiah declared,

> They say, if a man put away his wife, and she go from him, and become another man's, shall he return unto her again? shall not that land be greatly polluted? but thou hast played the harlot with many lovers; yet return again to me, saith the LORD. Lift up thine eyes unto the high places, and see where thou hast not been lien with. In the ways hast thou sat for them, as the Arabian in the wilderness; and thou hast polluted the land with thy whoredoms and with thy wickedness. Therefore the showers have been withholden, and there hath been no latter rain; and thou hadst a whore's forehead, thou refusedst to be ashamed (Jeremiah 3:1–3).

Ezekiel likewise used the strongest language to describe God's abhorrence of His backslidden people.

> Thou hast built thy high place at every head of the way, and hast made thy beauty to be abhorred, and hast opened thy feet to every one that passed by, and multiplied thy whoredoms
> (Ezekiel 16:25).

With such devastating evaluations of Judah, why is it then, that Israel and Judah were never designated as Babylon, and that God still sought to woo them unto Him? Surely this is evidence of the love of God. These were His chosen people; He loved them with an everlasting love, His mercy and compassion extended to them, even in the days of their most abominable apostasy. The love of the Lord for these rebellious people, who failed in so many tests, is remarkable. Note the compassion of the Lord in these statements:

> Say unto them, As I live, saith the Lord GOD, I have no pleasure in the death of the wicked; but that the wicked turn from his way and live: turn ye, turn ye from your evil ways; for why will ye die, O house of Israel? (Ezekiel 33:11)

After the Israelites had long since been taken into Assyrian captivity and the Jews were now in Babylonian captivity, still the Lord gave this message:

> For Israel hath not been forsaken, nor Judah of his God, of the LORD of hosts; though their land was filled with sin against the Holy One of Israel (Jeremiah 51:5).

We cannot forget the compassion that Jesus had for those Jews of His day, even though they were, at that time, preparing the final plans to take His life.

> O Jerusalem, Jerusalem, thou that killest the prophets, and stonest them which are sent unto thee, how often would I have gathered thy children together, even as a hen gathereth her chickens under her wings, and ye would not!
> (Matthew 23:37)

Ancient Israel and Judah, with all the privileges and all the knowledge that God had deposited with them, had failed in their mission, and God had eventually to reject them.

It must have been with the most heartrending agony that the God of the universe turned aside ultimately from His chosen people. Yet, right to the end, never is Judah called Babylon.

We must never forget that God did not turn away from Babylon. He ministered greatly even to these pagan religions. Every one of the great civilizations had its opportunity to turn to God. God so loved Assyria that two books of the Bible are dedicated to that nation: Jonah and Nahum. God so loved Babylon that through Daniel, Hananiah, Mishael, and Azariah, and more indirectly Jeremiah and Ezekiel the messages of truth came to that kingdom; and though Nebuchadnezzar himself was saved, never did the nation turn to God. The Egyptians had the privilege of having the Israelites in their midst, but they too rejected the religion of the Israelites. The Greeks had the opportunity to learn of the true God; Alexander the Great, fascinated by the Jews, especially the Jewish rabbis and scholars, worshipped in a synagogue with the high priest, but the pagan religions still prevailed. Rome had the greatest opportunity when the very Son of God was born into its realm, and the great apostolic movement under the Holy Spirit's direction took the gospel of Jesus to every inhabited part of the world.

Babylon was an idolatrous nation, and God abhorred its idolatry.

> Babylon is taken, Bel is confounded, Merodach is broken in pieces; her idols are confounded, her images are broken in pieces (Jeremiah 50:2).
>
> And I will punish Bel in Babylon, and I will bring forth out of his mouth that which he hath swallowed up (Jeremiah 51:44).

But so were Judah and Israel filled with idolatry.

> And they rejected his statutes, and his covenant that he made with their fathers, and his testimonies which he testified against them; and they followed vanity, and became vain, and went after the heathen that were round about them, concerning whom the LORD had charged them, that they should not do like them. And they left all the commandments of the LORD their God, and made them molten images, even two calves, and made a grove, and worshipped all the host of heaven, and served Baal (II Kings 17:15, 16).

Ancient Babylon and Ancient Israel

> For he [Manasseh] built up again the high places which Hezekiah his father had destroyed; and he reared up altars for Baal, and made a grove, as did Ahab king of Israel; and worshipped all the host of heaven, and served them (II Kings 21:3).

It was Babylon which destroyed the house of the Lord, the temple in Jerusalem.

> And he [Nebuchadnezzar] burnt the house of the LORD, and the king's house, and all the houses of Jerusalem, and every great man's house burnt he with fire (II Kings 25:9).

In doing this, Babylon had effected the physical destruction of the temple; but the Jews themselves had effected the destruction of the ministry of this temple, by perverting it into idolatry. In this they effectively performed a greater abomination than did Nebuchadnezzar and his army in destroying the temple.

> So I went in and saw; and behold every form of creeping things, and abominable beasts, and all the idols of the house of Israel, pourtrayed upon the wall round about. (Ezekiel 8:10).

> Then he brought me to the door of the gate of the LORD's house which was toward the north; and, behold, there sat women weeping for Tammuz. Then said he unto me, Hast thou seen this, O son of man? turn thee yet again, and thou shalt see greater abominations than these. And he brought me into the inner court of the LORD's house, and, behold, at the door of the temple of the LORD, between the porch and the altar, were about five and twenty men, with their backs toward the temple of the LORD, and their faces toward the east; and they worshipped the sun toward the east (Ezekiel 8:14–16).

There is a striking comparison between what was taking place in Babylon and what was taking place in Israel and Judah. Immorality, idolatry and murder indicated a total turning away from God, from His truth, and from His righteousness. It would be almost impossible for any casual observer to see the difference between the practices and purposes of the Israelites and those of the Babylonians. Yet God at no time called Israel Babylon, because there was a very small remnant,

> Except the Lord of hosts had left unto us a very small remnant, we should have been as Sodom, and we should have been like unto Gomorrah (Isaiah 1:9),

who, though difficult to find, unquestionably were the basis of God's patience, mercy and longsuffering to these evil nations.

The sin of Israel was far greater than that of Babylon because of the light that had been given. Yet it was also certain that the depository of God's truth was to be found in Israel, and not in Babylon. The absolute abomination of the state of Judah at the time of Jerusalem's destruction is clearly portrayed in the Chronicles. But king Zedekiah hardened his heart against the counsel of Jeremiah.

1. Priest and people sinned by following the abominations of the heathen.
2. The house of God was polluted.
3. The people mocked God's messengers.
4. They despised the words of God.
5. They misused God's prophets.
(II Chronicles 36:14–16).

Modern Israel is following the same pathway—ignoring great light to follow a mixture of truth and error. We are more culpable than those following Roman Catholicism, and we are more culpable than the Jews in Bible times, for we have even more light. But yet the distinction remains clear. Israel is never Babylon because:

1. It is the depository of God's truth.
2. It includes the precious remnant who keep the commandments of God and have the Spirit of Prophecy.

Because of the "very small remnant" in Judah, it continued as the one object of Christ's supreme regard until its probation closed at the time of the first advent. Equally the Seventh-day Adventist Church, though utterly undeserving of God's love and special esteem, will continue to be His special church until its destiny is sealed at probation's close. At that awesome sealing time every false and perverse element will be purged from the Seventh-day Adventist Church and it will become a glorious church, without spot or blemish. Thank God for that "very small remnant," without which our church would already have been as comprehensively destroyed as were Sodom and Gomorrah of old.

12

Modern Israel and Modern Babylon

Remarkable similarities exist between modern Babylon (Roman Catholicism, Apostate Protestantism and Paganism) and ancient Babylon, and between modern Israel (the Seventh-day Adventist Church) and ancient Israel. Recently the authors wrote a book entitled *The Road to Rome** in which they detailed the tragic intrusion of Roman Catholic practices into the Seventh-day Adventist Church. Undeniably we as a church, are retreating almost daily towards Rome. This fact has led many to believe that the Seventh-day Adventist Church is now part of Babylon. Such a conclusion naturally leads men and women to voluntarily withdraw their membership from the Seventh-day Adventist Church, and frequently to call others to follow in their tracks. There are those who have detailed in vivid language, the comparison between Roman Catholicism, its organization, its practices and those of the Seventh-day Adventist Church. Any honest, informed Seventh-day Adventist will be unable to disagree with these evaluations. The Seventh-day Adventist Church in the main has with bewildering rapidity, put aside its vision and purpose, its distinctiveness and uniqueness to seek the praise and acceptance of the fallen churches of Babylon. Such praise and acceptance will come only by compromise and accommodation to the practices and beliefs of those churches of Babylon.

Before we proceed further, the lessons that we learn from ancient Babylon and Israel must not be lost upon God's remnant church. As noted in Chapter 11, God never called ancient Israel with all her abominations, Babylon. Likewise there is not a shred of inspired evidence that God calls the Seventh-day Adventist Church, Babylon. Like ancient Israel, we are more culpable than Babylon. Indeed, we are held more responsible than even ancient Israel for our pathetic failures to follow the light that has so graciously been shed upon us. Concerning the failures of the Seventh-day Adventist Church the servant of the Lord has stated,

---

* Russell & Colin Standish, *The Road to Rome*, Hartland Publications, Box 1, Rapidan, VA 22733.

The failures and mistakes of ancient Israel are not as grievous in the sight of God as are the sins of the people of God in this age. Light has been increasing from age to age, and the generations that follow have the example of the generations that went before. . . . The reason we do not have more of the blessing of the Lord is that the professed people of God serve Him with divided hearts, as verily as did ancient Israel. They professed to be worshippers of God, but many as verily worship idols as did the Hebrews
(Review and Herald, May 21, 1895).

The same disobedience and failure which were seen in the Jewish church have characterized *in a greater degree* the people who have had this great light from heaven in the last messages of warning
(Testimonies, vol. 5, p. 456, emphasis added).

You are following the same path as did ancient Israel. There is the same falling away from your holy calling as God's peculiar people. You are having fellowship with the unfruitful works of darkness. Your concord with unbelievers has provoked the Lord's displeasure. You know not the things that belong to your peace, and they are fast being hid from your eyes. Your neglect to follow the light will place you in a more unfavorable position than the Jews upon whom Christ pronounced a woe
(PH117, Testimonies for the Battle Creek Church, page 58).

Therefore there is no group in the history of this world that stands more culpable before God than unfaithful Seventh-day Adventists. Yet we make a grave mistake when we assume that because of the astounding apostasy at all levels of God's work, that the Seventh-day Adventist Church is now part of Babylon, and therefore faithful people must be called out. The counsel of God is too plain. As we reflect upon the history of the Seventh-day Adventist Church we know some were calling people out of the Seventh-day Adventist Church not long after the failure of most of our leaders to accept the 1888 General Conference message of Christ our Righteousness. It seemed logical to these earnest people that no longer could the church be considered God's church when the leadership was rejecting that message which alone would bring men and women into the kingdom of heaven. Surely the time had come to look for another organization that would be obedient to the call of God, and to the counsel that He had given? How could a church whose leaders were rejecting the only message that would lead God's people homeward, any longer have the special regard of God? Clearly it would seem that the only way for the work to be completed was to evacuate from the apostate Seventh-day Adventist Church and join a new organization that would walk in the ways of the Lord and follow His Word. A number of apparently sincere men took up this position. Some used the Spirit of Prophecy to buttress their case. This was by no means new to our church. As early as 1856 there were those doing the same thing.

> Those who have published the Loud Cry tract have not consulted me upon the subject. They have quoted largely from my writings and put their own construction upon them. They claim to have a special message from God to pronounce the Seventh-day Adventist church Babylon, proclaim her fall, and call the people of God to come out of her, and try to make the Testimonies to substantiate their theory. These publications are misleading minds, and increasing the prejudice already existing, and tend to make it more difficult to get access to them to present the message God has given in warnings to the world of altogether a different character from the ideas presented in these pamphlets
>
> (*Review and Herald,* November 8, 1856).

Today we find the same claim that the Seventh-day Adventist Church is Babylon. Once more men and women are seeking to use the Testimonies to buttress their false propositions claiming the Seventh-day Adventist Church is now a part of Babylon. But this cannot be. The clearest testimonies of the Lord are against such conclusions.

> How dare mortal man pass his judgment upon them, and call the Church a harlot, Babylon, a den of thieves, a cage of every unclean and hateful bird, the habitation of devils, making the nations drunk with the wine of her fornication, confederating with the kings and the great men of the earth, waxing rich through the abundance of her delicacies, and proclaiming that her sins have reached unto heaven and God hath remembered her iniquities? Is this the message to bear to Seventh-day Adventists? I tell you, No! God has given no man any such message (ibid.).

Sister White outlines some of the characteristics of modern Babylon.

> This wine of error is made up of false doctrines, such as the natural immortality of the soul, the eternal torment of the wicked, the denial of the pre-existence of Christ prior to His birth in Bethlehem, and advocating and exalting the first day of the week above God's holy and sanctified day
>
> (*Testimonies to Ministers,* pg. 61).

Even in its terrible apostasy, it would be going too far to suggest that these characteristics were yet common among the members of the Seventh-day Adventist Church. Sister White gave many warnings against those calling members out of the Seventh-day Adventist church in her day.

> This delusion was opened to me. This is an intelligent man, of an acceptable address, and self-denying and full of zeal and earnestness, and carrying an appearance of consecration and devotion. But the word of God came from God to me, "Believe them not, I have not sent them!"
>
> (*Selected Messages,* Book 2, pg. 64).

> I attempted to show him that he was mistaken. He said Seventh-day Adventists were Babylon, and when we told him our reasons and set the matter before him, that he was in error, he had great power come upon him, and he certainly gave a loud cry. I sent to the office for Brother B—, and my son Willie who came in. Mr. B— stood up under a power proclaiming the loud cry of the third angel's message, swelling louder and louder. We had much trouble with him; his mind became unbalanced, and he had to be placed in the insane asylum
>
> (*Manuscript Releases,* vol. 1, pg. 298).

> My brother, I learn that you are taking the position that the Seventh-day Adventist Church is Babylon, and that all that would be saved must come out of her. You are not the only man the devil has deceived in this matter. For the last forty years, one man after another has arisen, claiming that the Lord has sent him with the same message; but let me tell you, as I have told them, that this message you are proclaiming is one of the satanic delusions designed to create confusion among the churches (*Testimonies to Ministers,* pg. 58).

Modern Israel and Modern Babylon

> The message to pronounce the Seventh-day Adventist Church Babylon, and call the people of God out of her, does not come from any heavenly messenger, or any human agent inspired by the Spirit of God   (*Selected Messages*, book 2, pg. 66).
>
> God has a church, a chosen people; and could all see as I have seen how closely Christ identifies Himself with His people, no such message would be heard as the one that denounces the church as Babylon   (*Testimonies to Ministers*, pg. 20).

God gives the clearest evidence that not only is the Seventh-day Adventist Church not now Babylon, it will *never* be Babylon in the future.

> Again I say, the Lord hath not spoken by any messenger who calls the church that keeps the commandments of God, Babylon. True, there are tares with the wheat; but Christ said He would send His angels to first gather the tares and bind them in bundles to burn them, but gather the wheat into the garner. I know that the Lord loves His church. It is not to be disorganized or broken up into independent atoms. There is not the least consistency in this; *there is not the least evidence that such a thing will be*. Those who shall heed this false message and try to leaven others will be deceived and prepared to receive advanced delusions, and they will come to nought
> (*Selected Messages*, Book 2, pp. 68–69, emphasis added).

Note some of the power of this statement, "there is not the least evidence that such a thing *will be*." It is not a matter of not being Babylon in the past, but the Seventh-day Adventist Church will not be Babylon in the future. Second, Sister White said that to voluntarily separate from the Seventh-day Adventist Church would lead people to advanced delusions. Many earnest people who have moved into this separationist mode are advocating one or more of the following delusions: (1) There are only two persons of the God-head; (2) Christ has not existed eternally; (3) we must keep the feast days; (4) Biblical prophecies must be re-interpreted; (5) God has given us evidence of an exact date when probation will close or when Christ will return; (6) we must use only the Hebrew word for "God"; (7) the International Date line should run through Jerusalem. These advanced delusions are all to be found among separationists and are evidence of the dangers of falling into this separationist thought pattern. Let us examine yet another unequivocal statement of the servant of the Lord:

> We see the unbelief, and the stout resistance of some who have had great light, and although evidence has been piled upon evidence, they have kept themselves in stubborn resistance. The Lord has sent messages of warning and entreaty, messages of reproof and rebuke, and they have not been in vain. But, we have *never* had a message that the Lord would disorganize the church. We have *never* had the prophecy concerning Babylon applied to the Seventh-day Adventist Church, or been informed that the "loud cry" consisted in calling God's people to come out of her; for this is not God's plan concerning Israel
>
> (*Review and Herald,* Oct. 3, 1893, emphasis added).

With the strong evidence before us, we cannot account for the number of God's people who have been trapped by this call to come out of the Seventh-day Adventist Church. This error has two major consequences, (1) the separator is in danger of losing his way altogether, (2) the separator leaves the Seventh-day Adventist church more firmly in the hands of apostates and the worldly. Surely Satan's greatest hope is to call faithful people out of the Seventh-day Adventist Church, the church that God has raised up to be His special agency, to take the everlasting gospel to the world. If the Seventh-day Adventist Church does not take this message to the world, no one else can, because there is no other church that is capable of presenting more than a small part of the everlasting gospel.

Satan's plan is to deceive the very elect. His purpose is to call people out of the Seventh-day Adventist Church, which he despises. That will be easy in terms of the half-hearted and indifferent, for when the final persecution comes they have no strength to stand and will quickly abandon their former position. On the other hand, it will take a more "noble" deception to convince "faithful" people to come out of the Seventh-day Adventist Church. Obviously he has set upon a plan; a plan that appears to call for a "noble" response to the abject condition of the Seventh-day Adventist Church. Thus, because of "godly reasons" and a desire to uphold "truth" and righteousness," people are abdicating their membership in the Seventh-day Adventist Church. Such a move will make it difficult ever to come back into God's fold because of their disillusionment with the Seventh-day Adventist Church. When God makes up His final fold, the majority of such people are unlikely to rejoin that fold, for they have developed hostility and contempt for the Seventh-day Adventist Church.

The message that God has for His church is not the message to come out of Babylon, but the message to Laodicea. This is a message that we must share with great earnestness with our fellow members. It is a message that, if properly presented, will wake many out of their Laodicean inertia to address the great needs that they have in their own personal lives. It is the straight testimony of the True Witness to the church of Laodicea. This is a message that comes from the faithful and true witness (Revelation 3:14). It is the message that declares that Christ knows our works (Revelation 3:15); that we are lukewarm, a condition which is repugnant to Christ (Revelation 3:16). It declares that we have an altogether inflated view of our own spiritual standing.

> Because thou sayest, I am rich, and increased with goods, and have need of nothing (Revelation 3:17).

The heavenly evaluation is entirely in the opposite direction, and the tragedy is that overwhelmingly God's people do not know this.

> and knowest not that thou are wretched, and miserable, and poor, and blind, and naked (Revelation 3:17).

Before there can be a transformation of God's people, there must be messengers who will spread the great message of the true witness, that will open before the people their true undone condition. Until that need is understood, there is no possibility that the majority will even consider addressing the pitiful condition of their spiritual lives. The faithful messengers also have the responsibility to share with God's people the beauty of the remedy that God has provided.

> I counsel thee to buy of me gold tried in the fire, that thou mayest be rich; and white raiment, that thou mayest be clothed, and that the shame of thy nakedness do not appear; and anoint thine eyes with eyesalve, that thou mayest see
> (Revelation 3:18).

The Laodicean remedy is necessary if we are to see a people ready for the kingdom of heaven. The message to be given, is an altogether different message from that given by those calling men and women out of Babylon. That message is the message to be given to the fallen churches of Christendom. The Laodicean message calls God's people from the depth of their spiritual destitution. God stands at the door of His church waiting to be invited in.

> Behold, I stand at the door, and knock: if any man hear my voice, and open the door, I will come in to him, and will sup with him, and he with me (Revelation 3:20).

God has declared that this Seventh-day Adventist Church is the depositary of His truth.

> God is leading out a people. He has chosen people, a church on the earth, whom He has made the depositaries of His law. He has committed to them the sacred trust and eternal truth to be given to the world. He would reprove and correct them
> (*Selected Messages,* book 2, p. 66).

> In this day, God has called His church, as He called ancient Israel, to stand as a light in the earth. By the mighty cleaver of truth—the messages of the first, second, and third angels—He has separated a people from the churches and from the world, to bring them into a sacred nearness to Himself. He has made them the depositaries of His law and has committed to them the great truths of prophecy for this time. Like the holy oracles committed to ancient Israel, these are a sacred trust to be communicated to the world
> (*Signs of the Times,* Jan. 25, 1910).

It is because of these truths held unwaveringly by the remnant of the Seventh-day Adventist Church, that this people is still the chosen of God. The Seventh-day Adventist Church cannot be Babylon while it has an unwavering remnant to live and proclaim this message.

The authors have met some who were introduced to the Seventh-day Adventist Church through a New Theology-type doctrine. Yet they have been able to find the authentic gospel of Jesus Christ in the Seventh-day Adventist Church. Either through contact with faithful Seventh-day Adventists or because of their own study they have realized the fullness of the message that God has given to His people. Those who continue to deny the clear testimony of the servant of the Lord on these issues will, tragically soon, openly reject the inspiration of the Spirit of Prophecy, then question the full inspiration of the Bible, and will eventually move into outer darkness. This is a consequence against which we most earnestly must warn, for it is happening already.

We appeal to those earnest men and women who have been misled into separationism to reverse that stand. Join with those who are unwaveringly loyal to God and His message; bring the light of the soul-saving message of Christ our Righteousness to the Laodiceans of God's Church and then take the everlasting gospel to those who know not the gospel of Jesus Christ. Such a response will thwart Satan's efforts to destroy the eternal hope of the faithful; it will allow God to pour out the latter rain in unprecedented power and will hasten the return of Jesus.

13

The Loud Cry Message Is for Our Church

Many earnest souls, aware of the astonishing entry of Roman Catholic practices into God's Church, have sought to proclaim the loud cry message of the fourth angel of Revelation 18 to God's church.

> And after these things I saw another angel come down from heaven, having great power; and the earth was lightened with his glory. And he cried mightily with a strong voice, saying, Babylon the great is fallen, is fallen, and is become the habitation of devils, and the hold of every foul spirit, and a cage of every unclean and hateful bird. For all nations have drunk of the wine of the wrath of her fornication, and the kings of the earth have committed fornication with her, and the merchants of the earth are waxed rich through the abundance of her delicacies. And I heard another voice from heaven, saying, Come out of her, my people, that ye be not partakers of her sins, and that ye receive not of her plagues. For her sins have reached unto heaven, and God hath remembered her iniquities (Revelation 18:1–5).

God's people have seen Seventh-day Adventist pastors join in Roman Catholic religious processions (*Launceston Examiner,* April 2, 1993). They have read the call of Seventh-day Adventists to join in sun-worship at the Easter sunrise services (Church Bulletin, Walla Walla Village S.D.A. Church, April 10, 1993). Believers have learned of the entry of Sunday worship, the proposed use of the blasphemous sacrifice of the mass, the proclamation of the false gospel of the Roman Catholic Church and sermons of the ministers of the fallen churches of Babylon within the sanctuaries of our Church.

> Special Ecumenical Service featuring the music of J. S. Bach will be presented in our sanctuary on Sunday, Oct. 9, 10:00 A.M. Father* Wolf, celebrant of Holy Eucharist; Father* Phillips/Matson, Gospel; Reverend* Tom Beck of Mt. Cal-

---

* "Father" is a title condemned by Christ in Matthew 23:9 and usurped by Roman Catholic priests.
"Reverend" is a title forbidden in Psalm 111:9, and used by Protestant ministers.

vary Lutheran Church in Sugar Pine, Preacher (*Bulletin*, Sonora (California) Seventh-day Adventist Church, Oct. 1, 1994).

In fact the priests sang a duet at this Sunday service in our church and the Lutheran minister led out in the Lord's supper. But let it be remembered that Lutherans teach consubstantiation—that the actual body and blood of Christ come with the emblems. It is a thinly veiled modification of the Roman Catholic doctrine of transubstantiation.

They have learned that Seventh-day Adventist pastors have attended ecumenical prayer meetings for Christian unity (*The Brisbane Catholic Leader*, June 17, 1990, p. 16) and of the presence of a Roman Catholic priest as an official guest of the General Conference at Indianapolis in 1990 (*Adventist Review*, July 13, 1990, p. 8). He represented the Pontifical College for Christian Unity and actually spoke from the podium.

Thus many now fear that the administration is taking our church into Babylon and the cry goes forth "Come out of her, my people." Sometimes that call is made in love; other times it is shrill and full of anathemas against those who still retain their names upon the membership roll of the Seventh-day Adventist Church.

But of a truth it is time long overdue that the Loud Cry Message be proclaimed *within* God's church. But it is *not* the Loud Cry of Revelation 18 which our God desires His people to proclaim to the Seventh-day Adventist Church, but the Loud Cry message of Isaiah 58.

> Cry aloud, spare not, lift up thy voice like a trumpet, and shew my people their transgression, and the house of Jacob their sins (Isaiah 58:1).

This responsibility the great majority of our pastors disdain. Yet each at his ordination took a solemn vow.

> I charge thee therefore before God, and the Lord Jesus Christ, who shall judge the quick and the dead at his appearing and his kingdom; Preach the word; be instant in season, out of season; reprove, rebuke, exhort with all longsuffering and doctrine. For the time will come when they will not endure sound doctrine; but after their own lusts shall they heap to

themselves teachers, having itching ears; and they shall turn their ears from the truth, and shall be turned unto fables. But watch thou in all things, endure afflictions, do the work of an evangelist, make full proof of thy ministry (2 Timothy 4:1–5).

The Loud Cry Message to the Seventh-day Adventist Church is a most unpopular one. Those few who shoulder the responsibility to present this much-needed message run a high risk of being described as critical and disloyal; and may have their ministerial credentials revoked or even their sacred ordinations "annulled." Church membership is likely to be placed at high risk.

It is time that we confess that we are "wretched, and miserable, and poor, and blind, and naked" (Revelation 3:17). Our church is in a pitiful state and it is time to forsake the ostrich syndrome which has overwhelmed us. The leaders of the North American Division were absolutely correct when they declared that "There is grave danger that the precious Adventist message will not be passed on to the next generation" (The San Diego Covenant published in the *Adventist Review,* March 7, 1991). Is it any wonder that faithful men and women, pastors and laity are anguished by the present situation within our church?

This is the time for the Loud Cry Message to be proclaimed in our church, a message for God's people to recognize their lost state and seek God's abundant grace in order to serve Him in purity of heart and obedience to His commandments. It is time for the Elijah message to be heard in our midst and its implications to be fulfilled in our lives. We must hear

> The voice of him that crieth in the wilderness, Prepare ye the way of the LORD, make straight in the desert a highway for our God (Isaiah 40:3).

It is time to prepare the way of the Lord. That can only be achieved when "The character of Christ shall be perfectly reproduced in His people" (*Christ's Object Lessons,* p. 69). It will most certainly not be facilitated by those who claim that they "do not find in Ellen G. White's own account any attempts to link the delay [of the Second Coming] to the idea of a perfect, sinless remnant" (*Adventist Review,* 150-year Anniversary Issue, Oct. 1994, p. 34).

Because "The day of the LORD is great and very terrible," God asks "Who can abide it?" (Joel 2:11). It is time for "the priests, the ministers of the LORD [to] weep between the porch and the altar" (Joel 2:17). What a contrast this is to the general jocularity of many ministers and the apparent lack of concern for the destinies of men and women within God's church whose lives appear to be totally destitute of piety and faith.

It is little wonder that our Lord commands,

> Blow ye the trumpet in Zion, and sound an alarm in my holy mountain: let all the inhabitants of the land tremble: for the day of the LORD cometh, for it is nigh at hand   (Joel 2:1).

That trumpet needs to herald aloud the warning within God's church, His "holy mountain." For those within God's church who fail to heed that trumpet sound, God will utter a terrible woe against these Seventh-day Adventists who claim to be seeking His coming, yet have been heedless of His call to thorough preparation in His power.

> Woe unto you that desire the day of the LORD! to what end is it for you? the day of the LORD is darkness, and not light. . . . Shall not the day of the LORD be darkness, and not light? even very dark, and no brightness in it?   (Amos 5:18, 20).

The Loud Cry to the church prepares the true in heart for the refining process without which none shall receive the seal of the living God. We are in the hour of God's judgment and this work is urgent; it is essential.

> Behold, I will send my messenger, and he shall prepare the way before me: and the Lord, whom ye seek, shall suddenly come to his temple, even the messenger of the covenant, whom ye delight in: behold, he shall come, saith the LORD of hosts. But who may abide the day of his coming? and who shall stand when he appeareth? for he is like a refiner's fire, and like fullers' soap: and he shall sit as a refiner and purifier of silver: and he shall purify the sons of Levi, and purge them as gold and silver, that they may offer unto the Lord an offering in righteousness   (Malachi 3:1–3).

This message of the Loud Cry to God's church must be given unimpeded. But today men in high office within God's church do all in their power to prevent the proclamation of this Loud Cry message with all vigor. Has nothing been learnt from divine history? from the record of the actions of the leaders of God's church at the time of the first advent and the time of the Babylonian captivity? Are we proudly declaring that

> If we had been in the days of our fathers, we would not have been partakers with them in the blood of the prophets
> (Matthew 23:30),

while perpetrating equal evils, oblivious of our own iniquity? Do we view our global mission as the destruction of this Loud Cry Message?

When Pastor Tom Turner sought to present God's Loud Cry message to His people in Fiji, the administrators of the church in Fiji, with the approbation of the South Pacific Division Religious Liberty Department, instigated his arrest and deportation from the country (South Pacific *Record,* June 4, 1994). When Russell and Pastor Turner sought to uplift the Loud Cry message in the Solomon Islands, similar measures utilizing the state were attempted with less success. (The full documentation will be found in *Remnant Herald,* August, 1994).

But no ecclesiastical edict will prevent the proclamation of the Loud Cry message, the Elijah Message, the Straight Testimony of the True Witness to the church of Laodicea. No ecclesiastical misrepresentation will minimize its impact. Today many Seventh-day Adventists tacitly accept the notion that God has failed in His promise to send the Straight Testimony to the Laodicean Church. Those who call for reform and earnest preparation to stand in the judgment, and who identify areas of sin in the church, are denigrated as evil, critical, traitors to God's church. Those who preach smooth sayings at this time of absolute peril are judged as worthy and loyal. How blind is Laodicea!

As in past crises in God's church we admire "watchmen [who] are blind: they are all ignorant, they are all dumb dogs, they cannot bark" (Isaiah 56:10).

The Loud Cry Message Is for Our Church

Thus "Peace and safety" is the cry from men who will never again lift up their voice like a trumpet to show God's people their transgressions and the house of Jacob their sins. These dumb dogs that would not bark are the ones who feel the just vengeance of an offended God (*Testimonies,* vol. 5, p. 211).

Rather our God informs us that

> I have set watchmen upon thy walls, O Jerusalem, which shall never hold their peace day nor night: ye that make mention of the Lord, keep not silence (Isaiah 62:6).

But the pleading words of genuine watchmen are ignored.

> Also I set watchmen over you, saying, Hearken to the sound of the trumpet. But they said, We will not hearken (Jeremiah 6:17).

Today God seeks humble men and women who will say,

> I will stand upon my watch, and set me upon the tower, and will watch to see what he will say unto me, and what I shall answer when I am reproved (Habakkuk 2:1).

Let each watchman heed God's dire warning,

> But if the watchman see the sword come, and blow not the trumpet, and the people be not warned; if the sword come, and take any person from among them, he is taken away in his iniquity; but his blood will I require at the watchman's hand (Ezekiel 33:6).

In contrast to those who reject their duty, the Lord will have watchmen who "shall lift up the voice; with the voice together shall they sing: for they shall see eye to eye, when the Lord shall bring again Zion" (Isaiah 52:8). Such unity will be found only among the true watchmen presenting the Loud Cry Message to God's flock.

Those who have a penchant to condemn the voice of reproof in our midst should study inspiration.

> In every generation God has sent His servants to rebuke sin, both in the world and in the church. But the people desire smooth things spoken to them, and the pure, unvarnished truth is not acceptable. Many reformers, in entering upon

the sins of the church and the nation. They hoped, by the example of a pure Christian life, to lead the people back to the doctrines of the Bible. But the Spirit of God came upon them as it came upon Elijah, moving him to rebuke the sins of a wicked king and an apostate people

(*The Great Controversy,* p. 606).

Indeed the Seventh-day Adventist Church urgently needs to heed the Loud Cry Message. It is a message for her. But it is crucial that a clear distinction be drawn between the Loud Cry message of Revelation 18 and the Loud Cry message of Isaiah 58. The first is directed to Babylon (the fallen churches of Christendom), the latter to the one object of Christ's supreme regard. To misapply these two messages may be an error with eternal implications.

14

Cast Out for Righteousness' Sake

It cannot be doubted that there are many who, tragically, merit disfellowshiping from God's remnant church. Through research of the Bible, we believe that we can find but two causes for such drastic action by God's church—those who are guilty of open and persistent violation of the commandments of God, and those who have accepted and are promulgating beliefs that directly attack the fundamental pillars of God's faith. Such pillars include the messages of Christ Our Righteousness, the sanctuary together with the 2,300 day prophecy and the investigative judgement, the seventh-day Sabbath, the non-immortality of the soul, and the imminent return of our Lord and Saviour Jesus Christ.

Outside of these two areas, we recognize that there are those who are not faithful to our Lord, but we must be ever careful lest we uproot any wheat with the tares. There will be those whose personalities and whose mannerisms will not be pleasing to us and who may present their burdensome concerns in a way that creates an unfavorable environment. But the servant of the Lord has very clear counsel concerning these people.

> Christ has plainly taught that those who persist in open sin must be separated from the church, but He has not committed to us the work of judging character and motive. He knows our nature too well to entrust this work to us. Should we try to uproot from the church those whom we suppose to be spurious Christians, we should be sure to make mistakes
> *(Christ's Object Lessons*, p.71).

These principles were well understood by the pioneers of the Seventh-day Adventist Church. They operated strictly according to the principles of the Word of God, but we have come to a position in our history where we have added and continued to add grounds for disfellowshiping. None were more dangerous than the additions made in 1980 at the General Conference session in Dallas, Texas. A review of the 1932 church manual, the first produced by the Seventh-day Adventist Church, listed but four bases for disfellowshiping. The 1990 Manual lists eleven.

Several of those that are now distinctive and individual grounds for disfellowshiping were combined in the 1932 manual. However, number seven, the one added in 1980, is the one that is often the basis of Church discipline.

> 7. Adhering to or taking part in a divisive or disloyal movement or organization   (*Church Manual,* 1990, p. 160).

The other most commonly used ground for disfellowshiping members is "failure to accept properly constituted church authority."

Most of the other grounds for disfellowshipment are objective grounds dealing with lifestyle and direct sin and apostasy, all of which can be clearly and fairly addressed. But number seven is wholly subjective. It leaves to the church members the responsibility to determine whether indeed the accused has been divisive, or schismatic, or whether he is causing disruptions within the church. It is far too tempting to use ground No. 7 to disfellowship anyone who in godly concern is seeking to redress apostasies and sin within his local church or the church corporate.

Today there are many thousands of faithful Seventh-day Adventists who are deeply concerned over such issues as the march toward ecumenical union with the churches of fallen Babylon and with the introduction of pagan forms of worship consistent with the New Age and the Charismatic movements. Others are concerned about pastors, elders, and Sabbath-school teachers who are with determination teaching a concept of "salvation in sin." There are others who are burdened by the infiltration of evangelical protestantism into the Seventh-day Adventist Church. Yet others are concerned by the entertainment and sports that are destroying the very fabric of our youth. Still others express their grief over the rapid decline in our educational, health and publishing institutions.

From the positive side there are those who are calling for the training of our members in service for God. Others are calling for preachers to teach the true Seventh-day Adventist message to our young people, preparing them to place Christ as the true center of their lives. Still others are burdened to distribute literature which will arrest the attention and minds of the community members so that they might be receptive to the glorious everlasting gospel.

Still others are anxious to hold Bible studies in their homes to help both Seventh-day Adventists and non-Seventh-day Adventists to understand the message of salvation.

It seems that many in authoritative positions are willing to oppose and even attack those who present their concerns and petitions. A number of people have discovered they are often accused falsely of being the "troublers of Israel." Yet, those who have used the kindest, most loving approaches have often found themselves in just as hostile an environment as those who may have been more direct and aggressive in sharing their concerns.

It has been discovered that, for many, there is no "right way" to approach these issues. Not only have people been placed under church discipline because of aggressive outbursts against the apostasy and those in apostasy in their church: others have been disciplined because of holding Bible studies in their homes and others because of distributing books such as *The Great Controversy*. Still others have been disciplined because they have sought to share truth-filled principles in their Sabbath-school class; yet others for street witnessing or for operating a radio program. In far too many churches, perplexed faithful members now find themselves accused of disloyalty to the church they love, have served for decades, and whose special truths they seek to uplift.

The issues, however, seem destined to become much worse. If the recommendations of the commission on world church organization are adopted at the 1995 General Conference session, then we can expect an extraordinary increase in the number of those who will be cast out of God's Seventh-day Adventist Church for righteousness' sake. In a newsletter sent to his church membership, Elder Gordon Bietz, then senior pastor of the Collegedale Seventh-day Adventist Church, now president of the Georgia-Cumberland Conference wrote as follows:

> The commission is more clearly defining the roles of the administration and departments of the General Conference. With the growing world membership, the General Conference session will soon be too large, and so recommendations are being made about limiting the number of delegates. Recommendations will also include electing fewer division personnel at a General Conference session and electing them at division meetings instead. The General Conference commit-

tee has been very large, and there are recommendations to cut the size of the committee dramatically as well as making it more representative of the world church.

The next meeting will be at Cohutta Springs [Georgia] in March, at which time there will be discussions of more tightly linking the organizational structure of the church. The net effect of such linkage would be to give the higher organizations more authority to prevent lower organizational departure from official church policy. That discussion will include a proposal that will allow a conference committee or constituency meeting to disfellowship a local church member that the local church refuses to deal with.

The world church is a very complex organization, and there are many cultural and national diversities to consider in making organizational change (*Church Beat,* September 15, 1993).

Each one of these proposed recommendations is cause for deep concern to faithful Seventh-day Adventists because they are, on the whole, designed to place authority and decision making in the hands of fewer and fewer people, thus increasing the likelihood of oppressive hierarchical decision making. However, it is the last of these that is most relevant to the dialogue of this chapter. Already in the South Pacific division, aggressive steps are being taken to implement this type of action. These proposed recommendations are in absolute opposition to God's principles that allow autonomy at all levels of our work; local church, local conference, union conference, and General conference. For a "higher" organization to reach down and to make decisions concerning members of a church is to violate the very essence of true representative governance established by God in the Seventh-day Adventist Church. Surely it is the members of a local church who are best able to decide whether a member has violated God's principles.* Even if the local church errs in its decisions, the members are the ones who have to live with their own folly. It is this fact which leads church members to a level of caution in matters of church discipline which "higher" levels of the church do not always display.

---

* See *The Temple Cleansed,* Colin and Russell Standish, Hartland Institute, Box 1, Rapidan, VA, 22733.

It is the hope of the authors that, resolutely and overwhelmingly, these recommendations will be rejected at the 1995 General Conference Session. But no doubt, by the time some read this book, the decisions will have been made and the reader will know what the outcome has been. We have friends and acquaintances in many parts of the world that have been cast out, not because of sin nor apostasy, but because of their dedicated stand for truth; men and women who "no longer consent to listen without protest to the perversion of truth" (*Selected Messages*, Book 1, p. 196).*

We have such friends and acquaintances in Great Britain, Germany, Switzerland, the former Yugoslavia, Poland, Hungary, the former Soviet Union, United States, Canada, Australia, New Zealand, Zimbabwe, and South Korea. These faithful folk are no longer accorded the privileges of membership in God's remnant church, not because they have chosen to leave the church nor because of sin or apostasy, but because they are being cast out for standing *against* the rampaging apostasy that is sweeping the ranks of God's people. Many have been proven soul-winners who, unlike many who have raised the hand for their disfellowshipment, have brought souls into God's remnant church.

We think of Pastor Korinth. Pastor Korinth was an ordained minister of a Seventh-day Adventist Church for fifty-eight years, who was an East German, suffering through the Nazi leadership and then the time of communism in East Germany, who remained a faithful pastor to the Lord.

Around 1980, Pastor Korinth and his family were able to move to West Berlin, when the West Berlin government paid 80,000 marks to the East German government for their liberation. His older son, Bernt, is an ear, nose and throat specialist. On their arrival in the west, they thought they had been liberated, and in the vigor and excitement of being able to follow the leading of the Lord, they enthusiastically sought out mission work. All the profits that Dr. Korinth made went into producing tracts, buying equipment, computers, printers and duplicators, all of which were located in the basement of his home. Teams went out on the streets

---

* As we go to press we have received word that the above proposal will not be presented before the 1995 General Conference session. If true this is cause for relief but not for relaxed vigilance.

distributing literature to the apparent embarrassment of the Greater Berlin Conference. Eventually they were told that the testimonies of their experiences were not welcome in the local church that they were attending.

Dr. Korinth discovered that he could purchase time on a Berlin radio station to preach the truth. He decided to give a quarter-hour message and invited his aged father to come into the radio studio to answer questions concerning the Word of God from call-ins. Because this work had not been authorized by the Greater Berlin Conference, they were told that it must cease. Neither father nor son could give up this precious opportunity to share the truth of the gospel. And so, both were disfellowshipped; Pastor Korinth, 83 years of age, 58 years an ordained minister of the Seventh-day Adventist Church, lost his credentials and his membership. What a tragedy! Today, well over 90 years old, Pastor Korinth, but not his son, has recovered his church membership.

We think of Brother and Sister Cabbin of Norwich, England. For more than fifty years they had been faithful members of the Seventh-day Adventist Church, joining shortly after their wedding. Brother Cabbin had been a long time elder, first of the Camp Hill Church in Birmingham, the largest church of what was then the North British Conference. He has also been an elder in the Norwich church following their moving to that location. Because they stood for the truth of God and attended meetings by those faithfully presenting the truth, they were eventually disfellowshipped from the church. Even more disgracefully, the letter informing them of their disfellowshipment requested that they find somewhere else to worship. The church notice stated, "This is a house of prayer for all. All welcome." But this proved untrue to this fine couple. Kindly, faithful people, they have led a number of people into the Seventh-day Adventist church.

We recall Garry Romano of Cairns, North Queensland, Australia. He was a man who all his life had had one goal and one goal alone, and that was to be an airline pilot. He had been brought up in a nominal mixed Anglican and Roman Catholic home, and at the time that he was confronted with the Seventh-day Adventist message, he was captain of a Boeing 737 for New Guinea Airlines. He discovered the *Great Controversy* in a motel in Honiara, Solomon Islands, and in reading that book, he became interested, eventually leading to his conversion to Seventh-day Adventism and the end of his golden dream to become a captain of a Boeing 747 for Qantas Airlines.

For quite a number of years he could not find permanent employment, but he remained faithful to the Lord and became an effective soul-winner. But when he stood for truth and righteousness in the Cairns Church, the North Australian Conference made strong efforts to have him disfellowshipped by the local church, along with Vada Kum Yuen, a faithful sister, the daughter of a long-time missionary to the South Pacific Islands, a woman who also is a faithful soul-winner for the Lord. When the local church refused to disfellowship them by overwhelming margins (37–17 in case of Garry and 51–4 in the case of Vada), the conference leaders persuaded the membership to disband the church, and these two faithful members were disfellowshipped by the conference committee, having been involuntarily transferred to the conference membership role.

At the instigation of the president of the South New Zealand Conference, the Rangiora Church disfellowshipped Brother and Sister Doug Hurley for no other reason than that they led out in a truth-promoting self-supporting ministry.

These are just a small sample of some of the reasons that faithful members have been put out of God's remnant church. But what a joy it is to know that God is faithful. And through Christ He has promised that these faithful souls, if they continue in their loyalty to Him, to His Word, to His truth, and to His righteousness, will be brought back into His fold, for they are still part of God's flock being driven out by unfaithful pastors, Conference and Union administrators and members. Remember, God has made it clear that in the end, they will have joy, and those who have cast them out, claiming it was for Christ's sake, will be ashamed.

> Hear the word of the LORD, ye that tremble at his word; Your brethren that hated you, that cast you out for my name's sake, said, Let the LORD be glorified: but he shall appear to your joy, and they shall be ashamed (Isaiah 66:5).

15
Church Discipline

At the General Conference Session in 1980 held in Dallas, Texas, a number of far-reaching decisions were made. The most notable of these was the voting of the twenty-seven fundamental statements of belief. Today these twenty-seven statements are increasingly being used as a creed, in the hope of securing orthodoxy among the membership of God's remnant church. Of almost equal impact at the 1980 General Conference session was the voting of an additional basis upon which members could be disfellowshipped from God's church. This is presently number seven ground for disfellowshipment:

> 7. Adhering to or taking part in a divisive or disloyal movement or organization. (*Church Manual*, 1990 ed., p. 155, "Self-appointed Organizations.")

From 1863, when the church was organized, until 1980 no such ground for disfellowshiping existed. Russell was a delegate to the 1980 General Conference session, representing the Far Eastern Division, and Colin was an attendee. We both immediately sensed the danger of such an addition. However, it was certain that most delegates gave little thought to the implications of this and voted it with hardly a thought to its devastating consequences. Today, especially in first world countries, article 7 may well be the most common ground for disfellowshipment from the Seventh-day Adventist Church. Alarmingly, it has been at least part of the basis for the disfellowshiping of many faithful Seventh-day Adventists. These are,

> the men [and women] that sigh and that cry for all the abominations that be done in the midst thereof (Ezekiel 9:4).

As earlier related, we are personally familiar with people in the South Pacific, Africa, Asia, Europe, and North and South America who are loyal and faithful Seventh-day Adventists who have been dismissed in recent years when their only burden has been to warn their fellow-members of the impending danger of falling into apostasy and sin. This trend in disfellowshiping is greatly accelerating.

It seems almost certain that this strategy has been either originated, or at the least endorsed, by certain General Conference leaders. We can look for large numbers of faithful Seventh-day Adventists to be dismissed because of their burden for the souls of their fellow-members; the desire to uphold the truths of the everlasting gospel, and to warn their fellow members of the dangers of accepting the specious apostasies of Satan.

We can further look for an acceleration in the disbanding of churches which refuse to submit to the pressure of so-called "higher organizations" which are seeking to force them to disfellowship God's faithful people. Such a situation within the Seventh-day Adventist church has been one of the most perplexing and disorienting events in recent times. This situation has led many to re-evaluate their former concept that in the sifting and shaking time at the end of the world, it will be the unfaithful who will leave the church, and the faithful will be in the church. Some have completely abandoned this biblical and Spirit of Prophecy concept, believing now that faithful people will be driven out of the structure of the Seventh-day Adventist Church, while the unfaithful will remain, deepening their apostasy and ultimately joining wholeheartedly with Babylon.

This has led many to assume that the time has come to leave the Seventh-day Adventist Church, resulting in an increase in the number of those who are requesting the withdrawal of their membership from the local churches of which they have been members. While we have a great sympathy with these folk who have been driven to this conclusion by the circumstances that have led to the disfellowshipment of faithful members including some of our dearest friends, we cannot support voluntary separation from the Seventh-day Adventist Church. There is no basis for such a move in inspiration. There tends to be a chasm between the attitudes and responses of those who voluntarily withdraw themselves from the Seventh-day Adventist Church and those who are driven out by unfaithful pastors and members. The Word of God should have prepared us for the disfellowshiping of many faithful members. Jesus said,

> They shall put you out of the synagogues: yea, the time cometh, that whosoever killeth you will think that he doeth God service (John 16:2).

Jesus laid before us the battle ground for the end-time. Satan, working upon the hearts and lives of apostate pastors and members, would drive faithful members from the Seventh-day Adventist Church. This is one of the master plots of Satan. His whole effort is to remove faithful men and women from the Seventh-day Adventist Church.

At present we discern three ways that this is being achieved:

> 1) The vast majority of unconverted members will be swept out of the Seventh-day Adventist Church when the persecution of the little time of trouble comes. They have no roots in the truth or in righteousness that would give them the strength or even the inclination to remain faithful when the Sunday laws are enacted, when the decree is made forbidding the buying and selling by faithful people (Revelation 13:17), or when the decree goes forth to put to death those who refuse to worship the beast and his image (Revelation 13:15).

> 2) Others will remain faithful to God's truth till the very last moment of probationary time. But having not allowed the Holy Spirit to transform their lives, and having not been broken upon the Rock Christ Jesus, they will eventually succumb to the evil one.

> 3) Others, so appalled by the apostasy and sin at all levels in our church, will conclude that the Seventh-day Adventist Church is Babylon and will voluntarily leave the Church, unmindful of the unfailing promises that God has made, in which He declares that He will sift and shake and cleanse His Church.

But the majority of the lost of Israel will be deprived of heaven because they have been led astray by unfaithful pastors. The Bible focuses tragically upon much of the carnage taking place and that will continue in God's remnant Church.

> Woe be unto the pastors that destroy and scatter the sheep of my pasture! saith the LORD. Therefore thus saith the LORD God of Israel against the pastors that feed my people; Ye have

scattered my flock, and driven them away, and have not visited them: behold, I will visit upon you the evil of your doings, saith the Lord (Jeremiah 23:1, 2).

My people hath been lost sheep: their shepherds have caused them to go astray, they have turned them away on the mountains: they have gone from mountain to hill, they have forgotten their resting place (Jeremiah 50:6).

Therefore, ye shepherds, hear the word of the Lord; As I live, saith the Lord God, surely because my flock became a prey, and my flock became meat to every beast of the field, because there was no shepherd, neither did my shepherds search for my flock, but the shepherds fed themselves, and fed not my flock; therefore, O ye shepherds, hear the word of the Lord; thus saith the Lord God; Behold, I am against the shepherds; and I will require my flock at their hand, and cause them to cease from feeding the flock; neither shall the shepherds feed themselves any more (Ezekiel 34:7–10).

In a dramatic way, we are seeing the fulfillment of these prophecies. The ringleaders in the disfellowshipment of faithful members have almost inevitably been pastors. It is true that they have been able to convince members of the local church who have little understanding of the truth and righteousness themselves, that for the harmony of the church they must disfellowship these members who are considered to be the troublers of Israel.

In the experience of the prophet Elijah, it was not faithful people who had troubled Israel, but the very apostates who were ready to drive away these faithful. So today, earnest members are sharing their burdens only because of their great love for God and for the very members who become their enemies in these disfellowshipings. With so many faithful people being disfellowshipped, and faithful churches being disbanded, it is altogether understandable that many have decided that this proves beyond all doubt that the Seventh-day Adventist Church as it is presently structured and organized has wholly apostatized from the Lord, and therefore the faithful members must withdraw all support and allegiance to it. But is this what the Word of God reveals? Far from it. In fact, we find in the Word of God the most encouraging words for those faithful who are cast out of God's church. God has promised that

He Himself will become the deliverer of His people, and will redress all the wrong that has been meted out to them by these unfaithful pastors and members.

> And I will gather the remnant of *my flock* out of all countries whither I have driven them, and will bring them again to their folds; and they shall be fruitful and increase. And I will set up shepherds over them which shall feed them: and they shall fear no more, nor be dismayed, neither shall they be lacking, saith the Lord (Jeremiah 23:3–4, emphasis added).

Jeremiah plainly identifies the faithful who have been driven out of God's fold as still recognized by God as part of His flock. The prophets Ezekiel and Zephaniah both support Jeremiah's optimistic prophecy

> For I will deliver my flock from their mouth, that they may not be meat for them. For thus saith the Lord God; Behold, I, even I, will both search my sheep, and seek them out. As a shepherd seeketh out his flock in the day that he is among his sheep that are scattered; so will I seek out my sheep, and will deliver them out of all places where they have been scattered in the cloudy and dark day. And I will bring them out from the people, and gather them from the countries, and will bring them to their own land, and feed them upon the mountains of Israel by the rivers, and in all the inhabited places of the country. I will feed them in a good pasture, and upon the high mountains of Israel shall their fold be: there shall they lie in a good fold, and in a fat pasture shall they feed upon the mountains of Israel (Ezekiel 34:10–14).

> I will gather them that are sorrowful for the solemn assembly, who are of thee, to whom the reproach of it was a burden. Behold, at that time I will undo all that afflict thee: and I will save her that halteth, and gather her that was driven out; and I will get them praise and fame in every land where they have been put to shame. At that time will I bring you again, even in the time that I gather you: for I will make you a name and a praise among all people of the earth, when I turn back your captivity before your eyes, saith the Lord (Zephaniah 3:18–20).

The message of the prophet Zephaniah pinpoints the time when God will redress these wrongs and will bring back into His fold, His flock who have been driven out. It is at the time of the solemn assembly. The most solemn assembly of the Jewish calendar was Yom Kippur, the Day of Atonement. We are now in the antitypical Day of Atonement. It is during this time that God has promised to redress the disfellowshiping that has been perpetrated by unfaithful shepherds and pastors. Those who are voluntarily withdrawing from God's Seventh-day Adventist Church are not mindful of God's sure promises. This is the time to exercise explicit trust in God's promises. It is almost certain that God will not bring back His scattered faithful until the shaking has been completed, at which time we can expect the faithful in Babylon to unite in one fold with the faithful in Israel.

Of great encouragement is the promise of the prophet Isaiah:

> And I will turn my hand upon thee, and purely purge away thy dross, and take away all thy tin: and I will restore thy judges as at the first, and thy counsellors as at the beginning: afterward thou shalt be called, The city of righteousness, the faithful city. Zion shall be redeemed with judgment, and her converts with righteousness (Isaiah 1:25–27).

Perhaps there are those who do not understand the phrase, "and take away all thy tin." Tin is the metal most commonly used in metal alloys. Thus, tin is an impurity, and God will remove all impurities from the lives of His people. Of great significance to every faithful Seventh-day Adventist is the twenty-seventh verse where God has promised that Zion (modern Israel, the Seventh-day Adventist Church) will be redeemed with judgment (justice) and her converts with righteousness. Surely these converts are those who have accepted the mighty call to faithful people to come out of Babylon.

> Come out of her, my people, that ye be not partakers of her sins, and that ye receive not of her plagues. For her sins have reached unto heaven, and God hath remembered her iniquities (Revelation 18:4–5).

At the end of time Jesus has promised that He will bring His faithful people back into His fold.

> And other sheep I have, which are not of this fold: them also I must bring, and they shall hear my voice; and there shall be one fold, and one shepherd (John 10:16).

Shortly after this promise, we have this remarkable prophecy of Caiaphas:

> And not for that nation only, but that also he should gather together in one the children of God that were scattered abroad
> (John 11:52).

Paul also confirms the fact that all of God's faithful people will be brought back together.

> And that he might reconcile both unto God in one body by the cross, having slain the enmity thereby: and came and preached peace to you which were afar off, and to them that were nigh
> (Ephesians 2:16–17).

It is within the context of this great gathering into one fold that the prophet Isaiah makes his declaration.

> The Lord God which gathereth the outcasts of Israel saith, Yet will I gather others to him, beside those that are gathered unto him (Isaiah 56:8).

The outcasts (those who have been scattered by the unfaithful pastors) will be brought back. But there are others to be gathered besides these. These surely represent God's faithful people who have for many years been ensnared and deceived by the fallen churches of christendom, but who now, as the loud cry of Revelation 18 is sounded, will also leave the errors and deceptions of their former churches and will join the one fold that God has established for His people. God is able to accomplish this in spite of the fact that in the same passage of scripture He indicates no change of heart on the part of the unfaithful shepherds who have been responsible for the scattering of God's sheep.

> His watchmen are blind: they are all ignorant, they are all dumb dogs, they cannot bark; sleeping, lying down, loving to slumber. Yea, they are greedy dogs which can never have enough, and they are shepherds that cannot understand: they all look to their own way, every one for his gain, from his quarter. (Isaiah 56:10–11).

We have carefully studied these wonderful prophecies of Scripture. It has given us the assurance that no matter how bleak or dismal might be the picture, no matter how many faithful members are driven out of the Seventh-day Adventist Church, that God has given a promise that He will not forget them. In the most pleading terms, we want to encourage those people who are treated disdainfully by unfaithful pastors, and who are driven out of their churches, that in faith, patience and Christian love they wait for God to bring them back into His fold. He has promised and He will not fail. Ever remember that during the time of your banishment you have continued to be securely part of his flock. Chapter 18 deals with places of worship for those cast out.

In the most earnest tones we address those who have or are considering voluntarily withdrawing their membership from the church. *Do not do it.* It is presumption to voluntarily withdraw your church membership. Put yourself in the hands of God. Let Him make that decision. If in His will, He allows you to be disfellowshipped, still praise Him and in contented faith wait for that moment when He will bring you back to His fold. We cannot expect this to happen until after the Sunday laws and the completion of the shaking when "all that can be shaken will be shaken" (*Testimonies*, vol. 1, p. 355).

Those who have oppressed you and claimed to be effecting God's work in so doing will not always triumph.

> Hear the word of the LORD, ye that tremble at his word; Your brethren that hated you, that cast you out for my name's sake, said, Let the LORD be glorified: but he shall appear to your joy, and they shall be ashamed (Isaiah 66:5).

By the close of probation all God's faithful, purified saints will be in one fold. We reiterate, the great fear and burden that we share is that many of those who have voluntarily taken themselves from the Seventh-day Adventist Church will at that time not recognize the call to come back into the church, for they may have developed such an antagonistic attitude to God's church that they will have no desire to rejoin the Church and will remain outside the fold for which Christ, the True Shepherd, will return.

Thus we urge the burdened souls of Seventh-day Adventism to respond not to their emotions nor even to their reasoning, but to respond to the clear testimony of Jesus Christ. He is the One who will redress all the injustices and evils that befall His people.

> To me belongeth vengeance, and recompence
> (Deuteronomy 32:35).

> According to their deeds, accordingly he will repay, fury to his adversaries, recompence to his enemies (Isaiah 59:18).

> For we know him that hath said, Vengeance belongeth unto me, I will recompense, saith the Lord. And again, The Lord shall judge his people (Hebrews 10:30).

This is not a time to take matters into our own hands, but to follow the counsel of Inspiration. Paul understood this when he wrote,

> Dearly beloved, avenge not yourselves, but rather give place unto wrath: for it is written, Vengeance is mine; I will repay, saith the Lord (Romans 12:19).

At this time when so many injustices are to be found, surely the Lord heareth the cry of His people.

> O LORD God, to whom vengeance belongeth; O God, to whom vengeance belongeth, shew thyself (Psalm 94:1).

This agonizing cry of God's people will be heard and God will answer this call. Let us with patience, faith and courage, wait upon the Lord, fully confident that what He has promised, He will fulfill one day in the near future. After the shaking is completed, all God's remnant will be brought back into Christ's fold along with the faithful who have responded to the call to come out of Babylon.

16
Organization, Structure, and Name

Among some of the greatest concerns of those who are contemplating voluntarily separating from the Seventh-day Adventist organization, and those who have already made the decision to separate, are the questions of organization, structure, and name. Many have concluded that the Seventh-day Adventist organization cannot go through because it is now securely hierarchical in form and therefore the present church structure, rather than reflecting the paradigm that God had chosen for His end-time church, reflects the organization of fallen Babylon. Further, the same people often ask questions such as, "Do you really believe the *un*faithful members of God's church will change their name from Seventh-day Adventist to another name?" These issues will be addressed in this chapter.

Whenever there has been apostasy in our church there have been those who believe organization is not important. Indeed, at the commencement of the Seventh-day Adventist denomination there was bitter opposition to the idea of forming God's people into an organization. It was felt that organization *per se* was Babylonian. Only the counsel of the Servant of the Lord was able to counter the strength of this movement. After the rejection of the 1888 message of Christ Our Righteousness by many of our leaders, there was strong agitation by some that the time had come to work independently of the Seventh-day Adventist Church. When the breakdown of the decentralized model of church organization came in 1903, that concept gained even greater impetus.* It was strongly voiced that each person had to respond directly to the call of God independently of any other human being. Certainly, this concept was strongly advanced by A.T. Jones and had a degree of influence, especially in the Washington, D.C. area. But at the 1909 General Conference Session a message from Sister White, read before the assembled delegates clarified the issue.

---

* See Colin and Russell Standish, *The Temple Cleansed*, Hartland Publications, Box 1, Rapidan, VA 22733, U.S.A.

> The world is filled with strife for the supremacy. The spirit of pulling away from fellow laborers, the spirit of disorganization, is in the very air we breath. By some, all efforts to establish order are regarded as dangerous—as a restriction of personal liberty, and hence to be feared as popery. These deceived souls regard it a virtue to boast of their freedom to think and act independently. They declare that they will not take any man's say-so, that they are amenable to no man. I have been instructed that it is Satan's special effort to lead men to feel that God is pleased to have them choose their own course, independent of the counsel of their brethren.
>
> Herein lies the grave danger to the prosperity of our work. We must move discreetly, sensibly, in harmony with judgement of God-fearing counselors; for in this course alone lies our safety and strength. Otherwise God cannot work with us and by us and for us.
>
> Oh, how Satan would rejoice if he could succeed in his efforts to get in among this people and disorganize the work at a time when thorough organization is essential and will be the greatest power to keep out spurious uprisings, and to refute claims not endorsed by the word of God! We want to hold the lines evenly, that there shall be no breaking down of the system of organization and order that has been built up by wise, careful labor. License must not be given to disorderly elements that desire to control the work at this time.
>
> Some have advanced the thought that, as we near the close of time, every child of God will act independently of any religious organization. But I have been instructed by the Lord that in this work there is no such thing as every man's being independent   (*Testimonies,* Vol. 9, p. 257, 258).

Now the above must be balanced by other counsel in this testimony. There is strong counsel to leaders not to control the individual workers who are led by the Lord (ibid., 259). Also in the same counsel is the following statement:

> At times, when a small group of men entrusted with the general management of the work have, in the name of the General Conference, sought to carry out unwise plans and to restrict God's work, I have said that I could no longer regard the voice of the General Conference, represented by these few

men, as the voice of God. But this is not saying that the decisions of a General Conference composed of an assembly of duly appointed, representative men from all parts of the field should not be respected. God has ordained that the representatives of His church from all parts of the earth, when assembled in a General Conference, shall have authority. The error that some are in danger of committing, is in giving to the mind and judgement of one man, or of a small group of men, the full measure of authority and influence that God has vested in His church, in the judgement and voice of the General Conference assembled to plan for the prosperity and advancement of His work (ibid., p. 260–261).

The General Conference in full session must be respected and shall have authority. Now many are in the trap of believing that this means under all circumstances decisions taken by a General Conference in session should be held inviolate. That is not what the servant of the Lord says. Obviously the General Conference in session cannot take the place of the Word of God. Should there be a conflict between a "thus saith the Lord" and a decision of the General Conference in worldwide session, faithful Seventh-day Adventists will always accept the Word of God. However, it is wrong to treat lightly or with disdain the decisions that are made in a General Conference session which are consistent with, or not in contradiction to the Word of God.

This counsel of Sister White, toward the end of her ministry, must not be treated lightly. There is no mandate for us to act as independent individuals. We should counsel together with those whom we know are doing all they can to be led by the Lord. The counselling together is not so much to get the opinions of others as it is to seek wisdom that they may have received from a direct study of God's Word and of the Spirit of Prophecy.

There is however, no mandate for dictatorial leadership or the desire of men to control other men. Leaders must be seen as counselors and advisors rather than dictators and rulers. So much heartache could be avoided if leaders would follow the divine principles of leadership as put forward by Jesus.

> But Jesus called them unto him, and said, Ye know that the princes of the Gentiles exercise dominion over them, and they that are great exercise authority upon them. But it shall not be

> so among you: but whosoever will be great among you, let him be your minister; and whosoever will be chief among you, let him be your servant: even as the Son of man came not to be ministered unto, but to minister, and to give his life a ransom for many (Matthew 20:25-28).

In today's church it is frequently not those in self-supporting ministry who resist dialog with their brethren, but those in administrative roles in God's church. They enact edicts in the first place such as the "guidelines" for North American self-supporting ministries, without the least counsel with those whose ministries are to be affected by the guidelines. Pleas that matters of doctrinal dispute be openly discussed at General Conference sessions are rejected. Pastor Robert Pierson's pleas to his successor to continue to meet with self-supporting leaders for counsel, after an initial meeting fell on deaf ears, in the latter years of his life.

There is another statement that has been wrongly used by those who would hold to a posture of quiescence in a time of spiritual crisis, yet it is also needed counsel for those who are inclined toward an overly independent spirit:

> There is no need to doubt, to be fearful that the work will not succeed. God is at the head of the work, and He will set everything in order. If matters need adjusting at the head of the work, God will attend to that, and work to right every wrong. Let us have faith that God is going to carry the noble ship which bears the people of God safely into port
> (*Selected Messages,* Book 2, pg. 390).

Some people conclude that it is not necessary for them to concern themselves with the apostasy and worldliness in the church. Someday, they reason, God is going to set things straight. While God has not lost control of the destiny of this church, nevertheless it is important for us to realize that God almost inevitably works through the human agent. We have been warned, for example, not to listen without protest. During the time of the alpha of apostasy, the Servant of the Lord wrote to physicians who had believed that they should not speak out against the sophistries of Dr. Kellogg, these words:

Organization, Structure, and Name

> My message to you is: No longer consent to listen without protest to the perversion of truth. Unmask the pretentious sophistries which, if received, will lead ministers and physicians and medical missionary workers to ignore the truth. Every one is now to stand on his guard. God calls upon men and women to take their stand under the blood-stained banner of Prince Emmanuel. I have been instructed to warn our people; for many are in danger of receiving theories and sophistries that undermine the foundation pillars of the faith
> *(Selected Messages,* Book 1, pp. 196, 197).

If this was the counsel given at the time of the alpha of apostasy, how much more strongly must it be heeded today, as we reach into the fullness of the omega of apostasy. But it is important to remember that there is no way in which we can right the wrongs. Our protests are important. All our efforts to warn and to entreat will however be powerless, for God alone can, through His angels, effect the shaking and sifting that is necessary for the establishment of the perfect church that He will have at the end of time. Feeble human efforts nevertheless are used of God to bring conviction and reformation to those who will allow the ministry of the Holy Spirit to attend their hearts. In 1905 the Servant of the Lord, in spite of the reintroduction of a more hierarchical form of church government at the 1903 General Conference Session, warned:

> The Lord has declared that the history of the past shall be rehearsed as we enter upon the closing work. Every truth that He has given for these last days is to be proclaimed to the world. Every pillar that He has established is to be strengthened. We cannot now step off the foundation that God has established. We cannot now enter into any new organization; for this would mean apostasy from the truth
> *(Selected Messages,* Book 2, pg. 390).

This is a strong statement. Some years ago one of the leaders of the Seventh-day Adventist Reformed Church approached Colin after he had listened to three of Colin's presentations and earnestly inquired how it was that Colin had not joined the Reformed Church. He believed that Colin was preaching messages that were consistent with the beliefs of the members of that church. For about half an hour Colin detailed to him some of the things contained in this book which had led him to reject any thought of joining another church organization. While having sympathy with the persecution and the unjust treatment they had received from some leaders of the Seventh-day Adventist Church, nevertheless Colin believed that wisdom would have dictated that these sincere folk wait patiently for the Lord to fulfill His promise that He will bring back into His one fold, His faithful flock that has been scattered abroad. Now, such a statement does not mean support for apostasy nor wickedness. Far from it! In 1908 the servant of the Lord described the situation very clearly:

> I am instructed to say to Seventh-day Adventists the world over, God has called us as a people to be a peculiar treasure unto Himself. He has appointed that His church on earth shall stand perfectly united in the Spirit and counsel of the Lord of hosts to the end of time
> *(Selected Messages,* Book 2, pg. 397).

Calls for unity, however expressed, must be rejected unless they are based upon a pure faith. Indeed, if all share a pure faith there is no need to cry out for unity, for unity will have been forged by the shared faith of the believers. The urgent calls we read and hear for unity within God's church are merely verifications of the fact that we do not share a pure faith. Those proposing a pluralistic "faith" within our church, believing we may be united in diversity of doctrine, are in reality the enemies of truth and obstacles to church unity.

Perhaps the greatest barrier to true unity in God's church is a blind loyalty to pastors and leaders. Multitudes believe that loyalty to God demands loyalty to church pastors and leaders. While this is true of faithful pastors and leaders, it is emphatically not true of pastors and leaders who are bent upon leading the flock away from the precious messages of truth and righteousness. In the most unequivocal way God has condemned such disloyalty to Him, built upon mindless loyalty to man.

> Cease ye from man, whose breath is in his nostrils: for wherein is he to be accounted of? (Isaiah 2:22)

The church will be perfectly united, but only in the Spirit and counsel of the Lord. The disunity that we experience in the church today clearly is the result of rebellion against the Spirit of the

Lord. The establishment of a coercive organization is the sure sign of deep apostasy. As step after step is taken to strengthen the overarching control of centralized leadership, the plan of God is being overthrown. Man is seeking to set up a structure built upon coercive control over those lower down the hierarchal pecking order. But we need not believe that this hierarchal structure will continue till the end of time. Indeed, the servant of the Lord spoke plainly on this matter.

> *Under the showers of the latter rain* the inventions of man, the human machinery, will at times be swept away, the boundary of man's authority will be as broken reeds, and the Holy Spirit will speak through the living, human agent, with convincing power
> (*Selected Messages,* Book 2, pp. 58–59, emphasis added).

God will sweep away the human machinery. The hierarchal worldly structure that unfortunately has encompassed our church, will not survive the final shaking. This event will come during the pouring out of the latter rain. This does not mean that at that time, when the human machinery is swept away and the boundary of man's authority is as broken reeds, there will be no organization. Certainly not! The organization at the end of earth's history will be the organization of heaven, built upon servanthood and ministry rather than authority and rulership. It is instructive to note the end of the above Spirit of Prophecy passage:

> No one then will watch to see if the sentences are well rounded off, if the grammar is faultless. The living water will flow in God's own channels (Ibid.).

This statement is consistent with God's counsel in the fifth volume of the Testimonies, pages 80 and 81. Frequently God will use humble, simple men to be leaders. Some of these men will not have had the advantage of advanced academic education, but they will be earnest students of the Word. They will be men whom the Lord can trust to stand true and faithful no matter the circumstances. The present structure is of the world, and therefore cannot survive the cleansing power of the shaking and the sifting. Under the latter rain God *will* reestablish His government according to the simple, humble example of Jesus Christ.

Now there is another area that troubles many. We have often heard it asked, "Do you believe that the unfaithful in God's church are going to surrender the name 'Seventh-day Adventist'? Surely in their deep apostasy they will still retain that name." We say, "Absolutely not!" At the end of time only faithful, courageous Seventh-day Adventists will unwaveringly uphold the name of "Seventh-day Adventist." This is a name that is pregnant with meaning for those who are faithful to God and who are loyal to Him.

> We are Seventh-day Adventists. Are we ashamed of our name? We answer, No, no! We are not. It is the name the Lord has given us. It points out the truth that is to be the test of the churches. . . . That this may be, we must look even to Jesus.
>
> The name Seventh-day Adventist carries the true features of our faith in front, and will convict the inquiring mind. Like an arrow from the Lord's quiver, it will wound the transgressors of God's law, and will lead to repentance toward God and faith in our Lord Jesus Christ
>
> *(The Faith I Live By,* p. 304).

There is power in this statement. Everyone who loves the truth and God's remnant church, will thrill to acknowledge His loyalty to the Seventh-day Adventist name and all that it represents. But it appears that as we come to the final test of God's people, as the shaking and sifting of the Seventh-day Adventist Church takes place, many will want to disassociate themselves from this sacred, holy given name.

> A company was presented before me under the name of Seventh-day Adventists, who were advising that the banner or sign which makes us a distinctive people should not be held out so strikingly; for they claimed it was not the best policy in securing success to our institutions. This distinctive banner is to be borne through the world to the close of probation
>
> *(Selected Messages,* Book 2, p. 385).

There are a number of matters to be noted in this statement. There will be a great challenge to the name "Seventh-day Adventist." Sister White would not have emphasized that this distinctive banner is to be borne through the world to the close of probation if the name was not to come under assault. There will be many among us who will not hold out this name so strikingly.

Already this is taking place. Colin was in an eastern European country, inspecting a new church reaching toward completion. He looked up at the wrought iron name on the front of the church. Though he was not able to understand the language, it was obvious that it was identified only as "Adventist Church." He drew the attention of the three pastors who were with him to this and they themselves were surprised that it did not bear the name *Seventh-day* Adventist. In the time of the implementation of the Sunday Law it will not be a problem to use the name "Adventist," for many Christians believe in the advent of Christ in one way or another. But it is the "Seventh-day" that will be unpopular. Those who do not love the Lord with all their heart and soul and mind, those who have yielded to the world and to pressure prior to the Sunday Laws will not stand boldly to uphold the name Seventh-day Adventist. For expediency they will eagerly delete the "Seventh-day" from the name and declare themselves to be "Adventists."

A most ominous trend has already developed. There are a number of places where some churches and schools have already removed the name Seventh-day Adventist altogether. Some former Seventh-day Adventist churches now are "Community" churches. This has already happened in Australia and in New Zealand. Examples include the Calvary Community and the Cornerstone churches, both in Auckland, New Zealand. The White Chapel in Melbourne, Australia is another.

It is sad to note that some of these community churches are offering services on Sunday as well as Sabbath. It is claimed that this is to provide a missionary witness to the community. But perceptive Seventh-day Adventists are not deceived. They realize that when the Sunday Law comes that the church will be open only one day a week and it will not be God's holy sacred seventh day. Satan is already setting up massive groups from the church to defect from Seventh-day Adventism and to reject its name. Whenever true and false practices are permitted simultaneously, it is inevitably the false practice which prevails, for truth can never associate with error, whereas error inevitably seeks to associate itself with truth that it may be the more deceptive.

The removal of the name "Seventh-day Adventist" is also happening in our institutions in Australia and New Zealand. What once was the Albury Seventh-day Adventist School is now the Border Christian College. The Adelaide Seventh-day Adventist High School is now Prescott College. The Whangarei Adventist School in New Zealand is now the Whangarei Christian School. Our own alma mater, Newcastle Seventh-day Adventist High School, is now Macquarie College. Hobart Seventh-day Adventist High School is now the Highfields Christian School.

It is essential that faithful Seventh-day Adventists resist pressure from church administration to desist in the use of our God-ordained distinctive name, which is disappearing from our churches and institutions. At this time it is the responsibility of God's true flock to hold our name ever higher. Threats of legal action, so contrary to Scripture (1 Corinthians 6:1–8), should not intimidate God's people. We, ourselves, do not look with favor upon the use of adjectives such as historic, independent, congregational, community or reformed as portions of our church's name. We are Seventh-day Adventists—no more, no less. But in claiming that name we accept a great responsibility. It must not be taken lightly, lest we defame it by our actions and be judged culpable in the hour of God's judgment.

Any thought that unfaithful Seventh-day Adventists will carry the name when the decree goes forth forbidding faithful Seventh-day Adventists to buy or sell (Revelation 13:17) is wholly unrealistic. There will be an indecent haste by nominal Seventh-day Adventists to abandon the name. When the decree goes forth that those who will not worship the beast and his image should be killed (Revelation 13:15), then there is no way that anyone, other than those who have daily surrendered their lives to the Lord, will have the courage to uphold the banner of the sacred name that God has given to this people. The faithful alone will fulfill the glorious prophecy:

> And they overcame him by the blood of the Lamb, and by the word of their testimony; and they loved not their lives unto the death   (Revelation 12:11).

> Here is the patience of the saints: here are they that keep the commandments of God, and the faith of Jesus
> (Revelation 14:12).

As we look at the issues of organization, structure, and our distinctive name we can only conclude that there will be organization at the end of time, but it will be God's organization built upon simplicity and humility. The present structure cannot go through because it represents a worldly structure rather than the true structure that God has prepared for modern Israel. Just prior to the close of probation the name *Seventh-day* Adventist will be carried only by the remnant of her seed which keep the commandments of God and have the testimony of Jesus Christ (Revelation 12:17).

An understanding of these facts will restrain those who are considering making a hasty retreat from the Seventh-day Adventist Church. We need not move in that direction, because, though God's church is now deeply into the omega of apostasy, the promises of God are sure and He will fulfill all that He has promised.

17
Kingly Power

When Colin was studying Educational Administration at the University of Sydney, a significant section of the course was given over to issues of leadership. He was interested in many of the issues raised. The professor, referencing a wide range of data, urged that there were only three major criteria of leadership evaluation. The first criterion was *structure*. Did the leader have the capacity to move the organization forward, developing it from its various aspects, guiding the financial integrity of the institution, having wisdom in deciding when to move forward, how to move forward, and how to maintain liquidity and cash flow?

The second criterion postulated was *consideration*. This related to the issue of personnel resources. Had the leader the gift of inspiring others and of being able to get the best cooperation from those who were in positions subordinate to him? Was he considerate in his handling of his co-workers, and were they able to sense that when they had needs and problems he was a sympathetic and helpful individual?

The third criterion was *authenticity*. This criterion dealt with the credibility of the leader, *the concept that the leader was genuine*. Did the leader genuinely believe in the organization and in its goals and objectives?

These principles, though derived from human research, are, nevertheless, of considerable importance in the ministry of faithful Christians. Perhaps, the most crucial of all is *authenticity*. Do we live and practice what we teach and preach? Do we have the integrity to be true to the Word of God and the Spirit of Prophecy? Are we faithful in our ministry in God's work? Would we rather suffer and be deprived than diminish the work of God? Are we free from egocentric and selfish objectives? Are we willing to subdue the natural inclinations of pride and avarice so that we might represent the meek and lowly Jesus?

If we have true *consideration* we will have a love for God and for His truth, there will be a burden for souls, a concern for our fellow human beings that will transcend the ego protection that would lead us to put self before others. Have we developed such a burden for the salvation of humanity that it becomes the all-consuming focus of our lives and ministries? Do others see our love for them and for their salvation as more than just another way to advance our own importance? Are we concerned for salvation and not simply for baptisms and for statistics?

The issue of organizational *structure* is placed last because those who have *authenticity* and true human *consideration* will be strongly motivated to guard the financial integrity of the institution or the organization. Such a one will seek divine guidance to recognize when forward steps must be made, where steps of faith as opposed to presumption are to be taken. He will trust in the Lord for His guidance, His help, and for the resources necessary to do the work that needs to be accomplished.

All these criteria are critical as we look at the issues confronting God's remnant church. There have been those who give clear evidence of lack of genuine commitment to Christ and to His service. While there have been those who have misappropriated funds, or perhaps through negligence, or some other fault, have allowed God's institutions to go into financial bankruptcy, we realize that we cannot always judge the circumstances that have led to some of these consequences. However, we do know that those who rest their whole confidence upon Jesus and trust in His leading, and who are men of prayer and earnest study of the Word, are going to have such a connection with Jesus that all things will "work together for good to them that love the Lord" (Romans 8:28).

The Lord Himself provided the most specific counsel as to how God's leaders should relate to their colaborers. We have not been left in doubt as to the relationship between leaders and subordinates. There is a conception of leadership that is common in the world, that is anathema to true Christianity.

The Lord was facing a very grave crisis among His disciples. The mother of James and John had come seeking the highest positions in Christ's kingdom for her two sons. Clearly James and John were strongly supportive of their mother's ambition, and they had confidently responded positively to Jesus' question as to whether they were able to face the bitter circumstances that Jesus

Himself was about to face. Somehow the other ten disciples heard about this bold effort by John and James, and they were filled with bitter anger.

> And when the ten heard it, they were moved with indignation against the two brethren (Matthew 20:24).

Jesus then preached the greatest sermon ever upon the subject of leadership, in which He preached the divine principles for all true Christian leaders to follow.

> But Jesus called them unto him, and said, Ye know that the princes of the Gentiles exercise dominion over them, and they that are great exercise authority upon them. But it shall not be so among you: but whosoever will be great among you, let him be your minister; and whosoever will be chief among you, let him be your servant: even as the Son of man came not to be ministered unto, but to minister, and to give his life a ransom for many (Matthew 20:25–28).

Such a relationship between leader and follower will bring, not only harmony, but true Christian power. Leadership is not an opportunity for self-exaltation, for rulership, nor dictatorship. It is an opportunity to serve and to minister. And such leaders follow in the humble example of our Lord Jesus Christ.

In 1894 specific instruction was given to conference presidents on this issue.

> The president of the Conference is not to do the thinking for all the people. He has not an immortal brain, but has capabilities and powers like any other man. And to every man God has given his work (*Review and Herald,* August 7, 1894).

Unfortunately, in the very early days of the formation of the organization of the Seventh-day Adventist church, the issue of unlawful authority became central. Those chosen for leadership had forgotten the words of Jesus, or perhaps were unmindful of them, and they began to exercise arbitrary authority over the pastors in the fields and the members in the churches. The Servant of the Lord made it plain that this was not God's way.

> God has not set any kingly power in the Seventh-day Adventist Church to control the whole body, or to control any branch of the work. He has not provided that the burden of leadership

shall rest upon a few men. Responsibilities are distributed among a large number of competent men
(Testimonies, vol. 8, p. 236).

As Battle Creek developed into a "Jerusalem center" of the Seventh-day Adventist church, the Lord's messenger wrote strong words on this theme.

> The kingly power formerly revealed in the General Conference at Battle Creek is not to be perpetuated. The publishing institution is not to be a kingdom of itself. It is essential that the principles that govern in General Conference affairs should be maintained in the management of the publishing work and the sanitarium work. One is not to think that the branch of the work with which he is connected is of vastly more importance than other branches *(Testimonies,* vol. 8, p. 233).

Continuing in the same line is this counsel:

> The division of the General Conference into District Union Conferences was God's arrangement. [This was accomplished at the 1901 General Conference session]. In the work of the Lord for these last days there should be no Jerusalem centers, no kingly power *(Testimonies,* vol 8, p.232–233).

The consequence of not following this divine counsel is clearly outlined.

> Organizations, institutions, unless kept by the power of God, will work under Satan's dictation to bring men under the control of men; and fraud and guile will bear the semblance of zeal for truth and for the advancement of the kingdom of God. Whatever in our practice is not as open as the day belongs to the methods of the prince of evil
> *(Testimonies,* vol. 7, p. 180–181).

Kingly power is most often exerted to protect the introduction of false messages and worldly practices into the church. When there is opposition to these false messages and worldly practices, those in authority all too often seek to quiet the concerns and protests of faithful members by exercising heavy-handed power.

> Plans contrary to truth and righteousness have been introduced in a subtle manner, on the plea that this must be done, and that must be done, because it is for the advancement of

the cause of God. Men have taken advantage of those whom they supposed to be under their jurisdiction. They were determined to bring the individuals to their terms; they would rule or ruin. This devising leads to oppression, injustice, and wickedness. There will be no material change for the better until a decided movement is made to bring in a different state of things (*Special Instruction Relating to the Review and Herald Office,* p. 26).

The servant of the Lord strongly condemned practices that lead to dishonesty and therefore to oppression. It is almost certain whenever oppression is used, it is because of apostasy or dishonesty.

The great and holy and merciful God will never be in league with dishonest practices; not a single touch of injustice will be vindicated. Men have taken unfair advantage of those whom they supposed to be under their jurisdiction. They were determined to bring the individuals to their terms; they would rule or ruin. There will be no material change until a decided movement is made to bring in a different order of things (*EGW 1888 Materials,* p. 1427).

This message was given in the 1890s to the then General Conference president, Elder O. A. Olsen. Obviously we have not learned from the testimonies to our church fathers. But God is watching.

There are not a few laity and self-supporting ministries that leadership have thought to ruin if they could not gain dominant control over them. But God has condemned this out of hand.

The Lord will never sanction the exercise of arbitrary authority, nor will He serve with the least selfishness or dishonesty in the dealing of men with their fellow-men. Yet these things have been manifest in the management of affairs in connection with the work in Battle Creek. Words cannot express too strongly the offensive character of the disposition to rule or ruin which has for years been revealed, and which has been strengthening by exercise (*EGW 1888 Materials,* p. 1357).

This "rule or ruin" mentality undeniably has contributed to the great sin in our midst.

Let no plans or methods be adopted in any of our institutions that will bind mind or talent under the control of human judgment; for this is not in God's order. God has given to

men talents of influence which belong to Him alone, and no greater dishonor can be done to God than for one finite agent to bring other men's talents under his absolute control, even though the benefits of the same be used to the advantage of the cause. In such arrangements one man's mind is ruled by another man's mind, and the human agency is separated from God, and exposed to temptation. Satan's methods tend to one end—to make men the slaves of men. And when this is done, confusion and distrust, jealousies and evil surmisings, are the result. Such a course destroys faith in God, and in the principles which are to control, to purge from guile and every species of selfishness and hypocrisy
(Testimonies to Ministers, pp. 360–361).

This "rule or ruin" mentality has greatly worsened as we come to the final confrontation between those who will render their whole loyalty to their unfailing God, and those who seek to put the rulership of man ahead of the principles of God. Sadly, such "rule and ruin" philosophy continues to inhibit greatly the work of God.

But the rule-or-ruin system is too often seen in our institutions. This spirit is cherished and revealed by some in responsible positions, and because of this God cannot do the work He desires to do through them. By their course of action, those who reveal this spirit make manifest what they would be in heaven if entrusted with responsibility
(Testimonies to Ministers, p. 280).

Thus, we are faced with the situation where humble, faithful servants are being borne down by the attempts of men who claim that their position gives them the right to decide whether or not laity can do the work that God has called them to fulfill. In Russell's presence, one conference president in the South Pacific Division stoutly defended his authority to dictate who could and who could not preach in his Conference, since "God's people have elected one to this office."

Yet God proclaims a curse upon those laity who yield their allegiance to human power and rulership.

Thus saith the LORD; Cursed be the man that trusteth in man, and maketh flesh his arm, and whose heart departeth from the LORD. For he shall be like the heath in the desert, and shall not see when good cometh; but shall inhabit the parched

> places in the wilderness, in a salt land and not inhabited. Blessed is the man that trusteth in the LORD, and whose hope the LORD is. For he shall be as a tree planted by the waters, and that spreadeth out her roots by the river, and shall not see when heat cometh, but her leaf shall be green; and shall not be careful in the year of drought, neither shall cease from yielding fruit (Jeremiah 17:5-8).

Lay people who flatter pastors cause these pastors much harm and lead them to believe they have the right to exercise kingly power.

> He who trusts in man not only leans upon a broken reed, and gives Satan an opportunity to introduce himself, but he hurts the one in whom the trust is placed; he becomes lifted up in his estimation of himself, and loses the sense of his dependence upon God. Just as soon as man is placed where God should be, he loses his purity, his vigor, his confidence in God's power. Moral confusion results, because his powers become unsanctified and perverted. He feels competent to judge his fellowmen, and he strives unlawfully to be a god over them (*Testimonies to Ministers,* p. 376).

The effects of God's warnings are soon to be manifest among God's people. Oh, that leaders would serve as God has ordained! The voice of the prophet sounds in our midst.

> Those who know the truth are to be worked by the Holy Spirit, and not themselves to try to work the Spirit. If the cords are drawn much tighter, if the rules are made much finer, if men continue to bind their fellow-laborers closer and closer to the commandments of men, many will be stirred by the Spirit of God to break every shackle, and assert their liberty in Christ Jesus (*Review and Herald,* July 23, 1895).

There is an even more dangerous result of the exercise of kingly power that has resulted in a very grave development in the church. Many have lost confidence in all leadership, faithful and unfaithful because of the overbearing attitude of many of those in authority. This result was prophesied by Sister White.

> The highhanded power that has been developed, as though position has made men gods, makes me afraid, and ought to cause fear. It is a curse wherever and by whomsoever it is

exercised. This lording it over God's heritage will create such a disgust of man's jurisdiction that a state of insubordination will result. The people are learning that men in high positions of responsibility cannot be trusted to mold and fashion other men's minds and characters. The result will be a loss of confidence even in the management of faithful men
(Testimonies to Ministers, p. 361).

Yet God has a wonderful promise for His faithful people.

But the Lord will raise up laborers who realize their own nothingness without special help from God   (ibid.).

Our burden is to see leaders after the mold of Christ and of the apostles; leaders who are servants and ministers, not rulers and dictators; ministers who will counsel and advise, not order and control. God has called for the reestablishment of the priesthood of believers. He has called for the ministry and the laity to work hand in hand. He has called for denominational workers to work hand in hand with the self-supporting workers. He has called the evangelistic workers to work hand in hand with the health workers. All these issues must be resolved if God is going to bless the work of appointed leaders. If leaders refuse to follow God's ways, then He will put them aside and bring humble, faithful men to take the leadership of His work.

No superiority of rank, dignity, or worldly wisdom, no position in sacred office, will preserve men from sacrificing principle, when left to their own deceitful hearts. Those who have been regarded as worthy and righteous, prove to be ringleaders in apostasy, and examples in indifference and in the abuse of God's mercies. Their wicked course he will tolerate no longer, and in his wrath he deals with them without mercy.

It is with reluctance that the Lord withdraws his presence from those have been blessed with great light and who have felt the power of the word in ministering to others. They were once his faithful servants, favored with his presence and guidance; but they departed from him and led others into error, and therefore are brought under the divine displeasure
(Testimonies, vol 5, p. 212).

Now is the time for church leaders and those leading out in self-supporting work to take an altogether different approach to their responsibilities, and for them to realize how to unite with the laity to finish the gospel commission. Leaders must not rule and laity must not allow themselves to be ruled. Christ alone is our Master (Matthew 23:8). To fail to heed God's principles will lead to the ruin of God's work and the eternal loss of both the leader and the follower.

18

When to Establish New Sabbath Schools and Companies

Especially in the western world the Seventh-day Adventist Church has never before faced the magnitude of apostasy that is being faced today. The terrible crisis that led to the alpha of apostasy, engulfed the very highest level of our work. It centered upon two men, Dr. Kellogg and Elder A. T. Jones, who had been chosen with Elder A. G. Daniels at the 1901 General Conference session to lead the denomination. They were ringleaders in presenting the pantheistic ideas that led many to waver from the pillars of our faith. Dr. John Harvey Kellogg and Elder A. T. Jones had united in an unholy alliance to use their profound influence and enormous talents to lead men and women away from the truth of God. The omega of apostasy is of a much greater magnitude than the alpha. We should not be surprised that some of the ringleaders in this apostasy, as in the case of the alpha of apostasy, are leaders at the top level of our work. Concerning the omega of apostasy, the servant of the Lord had stated that,

> The omega will be of a most startling nature
> *(Selected Messages,* Book 1, p. 197).

While burdened by the terrible inroads of the alpha of apostasy, Sister White went further,

> I knew that the omega would follow in a little while; and I trembled for our people   *(Selected Messages,* Book 1, p. 203).

That many would receive the omega of apostasy was also revealed to Sister White:

> The omega will follow, and will be received by those who are not willing to heed the warning that God has given
> (ibid., 200).

No one is immune from this apostasy unless he or she is wholly committed to God and fortified daily by the study of His Word. When we preach, upholding that the Seventh-day Adventist Church is still the fold of God, that it will continue as God's chosen vehicle for the kingdom of heaven; we face many anguished questions from faithful and dedicated Seventh-day Adventists as to what to do when their local church moves clearly into apostasy. In some cases this apostasy seems to develop rather slowly, and in other churches there has been amazement at the rapidity with which this apostasy takes hold. The questions are often extraordinarily difficult to answer. We have had questions such as, "If the Seventh-day Adventist Church is God's church and we must not leave it, what do I do in my circumstances when we have a pastor who weekly teaches blatant error from the pulpit?" We face other questions such as, "How can you possibly say that this is God's church when every church I know is deeply into apostasy? We know of no faithful pastor in our entire Conference." We hasten to say that it is not what we say, but what the enduring counsel of inspiration says that has validity. It is neither profitable nor wise to continue to listen to error that is not elevating week after week in the pulpits, nor fruitful to the experience of any one of us. Further, it is likely to becloud the conscience and cause error to be perceived as less offensive. So from our experience, here are our practical suggestions:

1. The first intrusion of apostasy into your church should be addressed immediately, whether it comes from the pastor, the Sabbath school teacher, or whatever source. There is no merit whatsoever in waiting until such error has developed and matured, for the longer the delay, the less possibility of being successful in meeting the error. Our first responsibility is to do everything we can to turn back the tide of apostasy in our church. We need to work employing the principles of Christ to seek to reverse any apostate direction that may have begun.

It is not reasonable to discontinue our attendance of the church the moment apostasy surfaces. Not infrequently the ones introducing the apostasy are doing it innocently because of ignorance, or because those in higher authority have recommend this direction to them. Following Biblical principles, start with the one or the ones who are responsible. Your attitude will be of utmost importance to the degree of success that might be possible. If we have been angered by what the person has done, let us pray for true love before approaching that person, for only in the spirit of true love for that individual are we likely to present our burdens in the most winning way. We cannot, however, shade or modify our concerns, for they must be given as clearly and as fully as possible. Make sure you do not take up the concern as a matter of your opinion, your preferences, or your desires. Rather present the clearest testimony from the Word of God. Help the one to realize that what is happening is contrary to the counsel that God has given and will lead to very dangerous consequences.

2. If the one or ones responsible will not listen to your entreaties, then you have no alternative but to seek a wider forum. If you are a member of the church board, that would be the appropriate place to address the forum. Your concerns will not always be judged from the perspective of the godly motives that are activating you to make the presentation, but nevertheless, after deep prayer, and consecration of your own life to the Lord, you have a God-given responsibility to move forward. If you are not a member of the church board you may request the right to make a presentation before the board.

3. If the board does not respond positively to your urging of reformational changes, then the matter must be placed before the church business meeting. It is our experience, from talking to many people in these circumstances, that only rarely are the efforts of such dedicated laity successful, but nevertheless, those efforts must be put forward.

Colin knows of two cases where laity have been able to greatly help pastors who had been teaching error. One case involved a pastor in Georgia several years ago who had been transferred from another part of the country and faced the immense confusion that was taking place at that time in the teaching of gross error at what was then called Southern Missionary College. The pastor was battered on both sides of the issue, and having not been exposed before to the issues of the New Theology in such a clear way, he was wholly overwhelmed by it. But by the grace of God, a dedicated young layman asked the pastor if he would be interested in understanding what was taking place, and the pastor, in humility, agreed to accept the layman's help. The pastor accepted the truth of victorious Christian living, and that Christ took upon Himself our fallen nature; doctrines that had, prior to this time, been vague to him.

On the West Coast a pastor attended a Hartland Bible Conference. In one of the meetings, Colin spoke upon the topic of the incarnation of Jesus and His human nature in relationship to victorious Christian living. At the end of the meeting, the pastor raised his hand from the back of the congregation and asked if he might speak. It will be understood by many that Colin was somewhat apprehensive about what he would say, but this pastor said, "If I had heard this sermon twelve months ago I would have said it was heresy, but one of the members of my church helped me to see the truth of this message, and I want you to know that what Dr. Standish has preached today is the truth on this topic." And so we urge our laity not to assume that pastors, or leading laymen, who might be seeking to introduce either false theories or false practices into the church, are necessarily motivated by wrong motives. In many cases it may be the result of erroneous teachings in the earlier experience of the ones concerned.

4. If all else fails within the local church, then there is a responsibility to appeal the situation to the local conference. Be prepared for conference leadership to support the pastor. This will be a normal response, even if the president shares your concern. Unfortunately however, many presidents will not only support the pastor, but also the error that he is presenting.

5. The time will come, if the apostasy continues, there remains no alternative but to leave the communion of that local church. The time for that decision to be made will be a judgment call. Some may decide earlier than others that their best efforts have made no impact, and that the church at large is willing to go along with the apostasy. It is usual for those with children and youth in the church to be in a position where they may need to make this decision at an earlier time. We cannot allow our children to be bombarded with error, or with wrong practices, for this can have deep eternal consequences. This is especially true when our Pathfinder Clubs and Youth Meetings in the church and at

Conference Camp Meetings degenerate into brainwashing sessions to encourage our youth to blasphemous and secular worship practices and unholy social activities.

6. Once the decision has been made that no longer can we attend that local church, then we need to seek another church in the area where we are located where truth is upheld and taught. In some cases members of a church have been able to find a pastor and a congregation who are upholding truth. Such a church could be a safe haven for you, but keep in mind that pastors change, and often with the change of pastors, dramatic changes take place in the church itself.

7. Sadly however, we have heard the testimony of many people who have searched their area and have not been able to find another church within reasonable driving distance where week by week they can confidently expect to have their souls fed in an atmosphere of church fellowship that will strengthen them for the coming duties of the week ahead. It is usual that it is not just one family that recognizes this problem. At this point it is prudent to move to step eight.

8. In this step, those who are concerned, should seek to establish a branch Sabbath School in an area sufficiently distant from established Seventh-day Adventist Churches that it can be a light for missionary and soul winning endeavor. If a church board will not agree to sponsor the branch Sabbath School, seek another church. We have seen success in this approach in the South Eastern California Conference, and it has proved to be a blessing. However, it is possible that no church will agree to spawn such branch Sabbath School. We would emphasize that this step should be taken only after much prayer and study of God's Word. It is not to be taken because of anger at personal insult or mistreatment. It may only be blessed of God if adopted for worthy reasons. There are no grounds for hasty action.

9. If no church will sponsor a branch Sabbath School, you have no alternative but to move to establish a meeting place with no direct connection with denominational sources, but where each week truth and righteousness will be upheld. Sometimes faithful groups have decided to have meetings Sabbath afternoon so as to

minimize the perceived conflict with the local church. Others see wisdom in having services at normal Sabbath morning hours. Neither decision necessitates that you remove your name from church membership of the church of your previous attendance, but you will understand that you run the risk that in the not too distant future, your name will be involuntarily removed from church membership. Yet, we believe that you have done what God has asked you to do, and what are the only reasonable steps you can take.

If you have followed each of these steps, you have done everything you can, except compromise the truth; and we believe that God will honor your faithful decisions. But whatever is established, make sure it is not simply an in-reach, but there is an aggressive outreach into the community where souls are presented with the three angels' messages, and the soon coming of Jesus, challenging them concerning the preparation that they must have for the return of Jesus Christ. To be "Seventh-day Adventist" is to be evangelistic.

Care must be taken in establishing such entities for there are untold pitfalls and Satan is sure to exert every effort to destroy these companies. Too often we permit our selfish inclinations to aid and abet the archdeceiver in his designs. To stand against apostasy in God's church and not drift along with the tide requires men and women of firm resolve and strong wills. So long as these wills are kept under the control of the Holy Spirit, the individual is a blessing to the company. But that same person will become a curse if he or she permits an unconverted, egocentric will to control. We must ever stand strongly for truth, but yield to the desire of the majority in non-salvation matters.

Some pitfalls we have noticed deserve identification. These include,

1. Condemnation of those who still believe they can be a witness to their local church and continue in its fellowship.

2. The introduction of harsh rules in order to preserve the purity of the faith.

3. The use of the same dictatorial power by the company leaders as that which they abhorred in the organized church.

4. A tendency to become insular and to overlook outreach.

5. As time passes, in some there tends to be experienced a growing alienation from the Seventh-day Adventist community of believers rather than a greater love and desire to help God's flock to prepare for His return.

6. A sense of self-sufficiency in the belief that by comparison with those in the regular church their Christian experience is superior, thus losing sight of our hopeless state without the grace of Christ and our need to measure oneself by His life rather than the lives of our fellow Seventh-day Adventists.

7. A desire to form some type of structural organization with other like-minded companies, ignoring the counsel of inspiration. These companies will have fellowship together to support one another, but they should not form a new church organization.

Never forget that you will remain a part of the worldwide Seventh-day Adventist Church, and ever designate yourself and your little company of believers as such. Do not seek to join another organization. Never forget that you are part of God's flock and never forget that He has promised to bring you back to His fold. He will not leave you nor will He forget you. Soon, very soon, with all living saints you will be in the one fold God has prepared as a sanctuary for His people during the time of Jacob's trouble.

the written word

The spoken word is subject to the vagaries of myth and memory; only the written word endures. The earliest known writing dates back some five thousand years. Only since then has man been able to establish a reliable record of his history.

This fascinating book tells how the hieroglyphic Rosetta stone was deciphered by the great Champollion; how the Old Persian cuneiform characters were deciphered chiefly through the efforts of H. C. Rawlinson. It points out the many surprises that were in store for the readers of ancient writings—a hymn to Aton by the Pharaoh Ikhnaton appears among the Psalms of David; the Book of Genesis was derived from Ugaritic (Canaanite) literature.

P. E. Cleator traces the relationship of seemingly unrelated languages. His book affords an intriguing glimpse of the cryptologist and his work—the inspired guesses, the slender clues, the deductive reasoning, the apparently unrelated facts. Here are all the ingredients of a detective story. Here is the full romance of the written word, one of the highest accomplishments of civilization.

MENTOR Books of Related Interest

THE ANVIL OF CIVILIZATION *by Leonard Cottrell*
An archeological history of the Mediterranean, revealing the long-buried secrets of the early Egyptians, Hittites, Sumerians, Assyrians, Babylonians, Greeks and Jews. (#MP413—60¢)

WORLD OF THE MAYA *by Victor W. von Hagen*
A history of the mysterious Mayas and their resplendent civilization that blossomed in the jungles of Central America. (#MP394—60¢)

THE ORIGINS OF ORIENTAL CIVILIZATION
by Walter A. Fairservis, Jr.
An archaeological and anthropological study of the beginnings of culture in China, Korea, Japan, Mongolia, and Manchuria. (#MD251—50¢)

THE ANCIENT MYTHS *by Norma Lorre Goodrich*
A vivid retelling of the great myths of Greece, Egypt, India, Persia, Crete, Sumer, and Rome.
(#MD313—50¢)

TO OUR READERS

We welcome your request for our free catalog of SIGNET and MENTOR Books. If your dealer does not have the books you want, you may order them by mail, enclosing the list price plus 5¢ a copy to cover mailing. The New American Library of World Literature, Inc., P.O. Box 2310, Grand Central Station, New York 17, New York.